Roderick G. MacBeth

The Making of the Canadian West

Roderick G. MacBeth

The Making of the Canadian West

ISBN/EAN: 9783337186579

Printed in Europe, USA, Canada, Australia, Japan

Cover: Foto ©ninafisch / pixelio.de

More available books at **www.hansebooks.com**

THE MAKING OF THE CANADIAN WEST,

BEING THE

REMINISCENCES OF AN EYE-WITNESS.

BY

REV. R. G. MacBETH, M.A.,

Pastor of Augustine Church, Winnipeg; Author of "The Selkirk Settlers in Real Life," etc.

With Portraits and Illustrations.

TORONTO:
WILLIAM BRIGGS,
Wesley Buildings.

Montreal: C. W. COATES.   Halifax: S. F. HUESTIS.
1898.

ENTERED according to Act of the Parliament of Canada, in the year one thousand eight hundred and ninety-eight, by WILLIAM BRIGGS, at the Department of Agriculture.

PREFACE.

When the few short papers on the first colony in the North-West were put into book-form, under the title of "The Selkirk Settlers in Real Life," the book received a welcome far beyond its intrinsic deserts, because it gave some idea of how the early settlers lived in their homes rather than the ordinary history of contemporary events. Letters received from readers far and near, as well as verbal communications, have given me to feel that people are anxious to get glimpses of the moving actors in the human drama as an aid to understanding the events commonly known as the history of the country.

Hence, many who took deep interest in the simple story of the early colony on the Red River, were anxious that a record of the life succeeding those early days should be written by some one who was an eye-witness of the change from the old life to the new, as well as of the subsequent stirring events in the formative period of Western history. In answer to these requests, and with a desire to preserve a life-story of the land in which I was born and in which I have thus far spent my life, these chapters have been written. I have had neither the time nor the desire to write a compendium of all the events that have transpired in the country, nor to give minute details of all I have mentioned. I have sought rather to dwell upon men and events only so far as a record of them seemed to me to be relevant to my purpose, as expressed in the title of this book. I have simply gone back and lived through the past again, seeing the faces and hearing the voices of other days, and what I have seen and heard I have herein written.

It is hoped that the present work will give a sufficiently succinct account of the progress of the country through its formative stages, and at the same time have enough of personal reminiscence about it to make the dry bones of history more palatable to the taste of the ordinary reader than they might otherwise be.

Should it appear to some that certain things they deem of importance have been omitted, such will kindly bear in mind the scope this book contemplates, and they can fill out the incompleteness by themselves taking up the pen and traversing fields which this work does not occupy. It is in such way after all that a complete history is secured, for every man has his own peculiar point of view, if he has realized the meaning of individuality. The Canadian West has little more than begun a great history.

We who have lived here always have but heard by anticipation,

> ". . . the tread of pioneers
> Of nations yet to be,
> The first low wash of waves where yet
> Shall roll a human sea "—

and perhaps the present writing by one who was at the very beginning may be of interest.

R. G. MacBeth.

Winnipeg, April, 1898.

CONTENTS.

CHAPTER I.
Musings on the Old 11

CHAPTER II.
The Pathos and Peril of Change 19

CHAPTER III.
Armed Rebellion 32

CHAPTER IV.
The Plot Thickens 40

CHAPTER V.
Some Counter-Efforts and Their Results . . . 55

CHAPTER VI.
Collapse of the Rebellion 73

CHAPTER VII.
The Making of a Province 89

CHAPTER VIII.
Contact with the Outside World - - - - 115

CHAPTER IX.
A "Boom" and Another Rebellion - - - - 134

CHAPTER X.
Campaigning on the Prairies - - - - - 153

CHAPTER XI.
Rebellion at an End - - - - - - - 177

CHAPTER XII.
Religious and Educational Development - - - 209

PORTRAITS AND ILLUSTRATIONS.

	PAGE
LORD STRATHCONA AND MOUNT ROYAL (Donald A. Smith) - - - - - - *Frontispiece*.	
OLD FORT EDMONTON - - - - - - -	19
LOUIS RIEL - - - - - - - -	35
AMBROISE LEPINE - - - - - -	44
HON. A. G. B. BANNATYNE - - - - -	53
JAMES ROSS - - - - - - - -	67
SENATOR SUTHERLAND - - - - - -	70
RIEL AND HIS COUNCIL (1869-70) - - -	73
LORD WOLSELEY - - - - - - -	86
GROUP OF EARLY GOVERNORS: Hon. A. G. Archibald, Hon. Alex. Morris, Hon. David Laird, and Sir John Schultz - - - - - -	89
HON. DONALD GUNN - - - - - -	100
HON. JOHN NORQUAY - - - - - -	102
F. H. FRANCIS, M.P.P. - - - - -	108
HON. JOSEPH MARTIN, Q.C. - - - -	110
REV. GEORGE MCDOUGALL - - - -	114
LORD DUFFERIN - - - - - - -	118

	PAGE
HON. THOMAS GREENWAY	134
HON. EDGAR DEWDNEY	139
GABRIEL DUMONT	146
LIEUT.-COL. OSBORNE SMITH	151
NORTH-WEST LEGISLATIVE ASSEMBLY, 1886	153
CHIEF CROWFOOT	157
INTERIOR OF HUDSON'S BAY CO.'S FORT AT EDMONTON	164
GROUP OF OFFICERS, CANADIAN FORCES, 1885: General Middleton, Major-General Strange, Lieut.-Col. Otter, and Major Steele	165
INTERIOR OF FORT PITT JUST BEFORE REBELLION OF 1885	174
CHIEF POUNDMAKER	186
RIEL'S COUNCILLORS IN 1885	187
TOM HOURIE, SCOUT	188
HON. HUGH JOHN MACDONALD, Q.C.	201
LIEUT.-COL. WILLIAMS	202
GROUP OF PIONEER CLERGYMEN: Archbishop Taché, Archbishop Machray, Rev. John Black, D.D., and Rev. George Young, D.D.	209
REV. GEORGE BRYCE, LL.D.	216
HON. CLIFFORD SIFTON	221
HON. F. W. G. HAULTAIN	223
D. J. GOGGIN, M.A.	226
HON. GILBERT MCMICKEN	227

THE MAKING OF THE CANADIAN WEST.

CHAPTER I.

MUSINGS ON THE OLD.

It was not to be expected that the great domain of British America west of the inland sea of Superior would remain for an indefinitely long period under the sway of a fur-trading company, however paternal and beneficent to those under its care that sovereignty might be. Nor was it likely that the westward course of empire would fail to extend over the vast area which has been aptly described as the very home of the wheat plant, and which has become in its several parts the great producer of the staff of life, the grazing ground for innumerable herds, as well as the cynosure on which the eyes of the mineral-seeking world are now fixed. I never have had any sympathy with the somewhat generally accepted view that the Hudson's Bay Company, who since the year 1670 had partially, and from 1821 had absolutely, controlled most of this wide region, was the determined and active opponent of its settlement and progress.

Lord Strathcona and Mount Royal (Donald A. Smith), in his excellent preface to my former book on "The Selkirk Settlers in Real Life," puts the matter in such capital form that I cannot do better than reproduce here his paragraph on the point: "It has been the custom," says His Lordship, "to describe the Hudson's Bay Company as an opponent of individual settlement and of colonization. To enter into a controversy upon this point is not my purpose, but it may be proper to state that the condition of affairs at the time in question in the country between Lake Superior and the Rocky Mountains does not appear to have been sufficiently appreciated. Owing to the difficulty of access and egress, colonization in what is now Manitoba and the North-West Territories could not have taken place to any extent. Of necessity, also, the importation of the commodities required in connection with its agricultural development would have been exceptionally expensive, while, on the other hand, the cost of transportation of its possible exports must have been so great as to render competition with countries more favorably situated at the moment difficult if not impossible. The justice of these contentions will be at once realized when it is remembered that the Red River valley was situated in the centre of the continent, one thousand miles away in any direction from settled districts. . . . Personally, it is my opinion that the acquisition and development of the Hudson Bay Territory was impossible prior to the confederation of the Dominion. No less a body than united Canada could have acquired and administered so large a domain, or have undertaken the construction of railways, without which its development could only have been slow and uncertain. It was not until 1878, eight years after the transfer, that Winnipeg first received railway communication through the United States. Three or four more years elapsed before the completion of the line to Lake Superior, and it was only late in 1885— sixteen years after the Hudson's Bay Company relinquished their charter—that the Canadian Pacific Railway was completed from ocean to ocean, and Manitoba and the North-West Territories were placed in direct and regular communication with the different parts of the Dominion."

In addition to what His Lordship thus tells us, in a statement whose form and contents will commend it to every sensible person who is at all cognizant of the conditions referred to therein, it remains to be said, from the standpoint of the people who then lived in the country, that so far as my recollection and information go, they made no active effort to remove what might be called by some the "invidious bar" of their isolation, if we except the action of a few of the adventurer class—a class always ready to exploit frontier communities for their own glory. Why should it be reasonably thought that the people of that time, along the banks of the Red and Assiniboine rivers and out on the great plains, would make any special effort to bring in the flood of that larger life which, from the older settled portions of the continent, was beginning to beat up against their borders? The conditions under which those people lived were for the most part the best they knew, and, speaking generally, they were contented and happy under the *regime* of the Hudson's Bay Company, especially as that company did not latterly insist on monopoly in trade. The community, before the transfer, might be roughly divided into two classes, if we except those who during the sixties had come from without into their midst.

The Selkirk settlers and those of their class (who composed the one part) would not, so far at least as the older generation was concerned, be eager for more struggles and wrenchings. For years after coming to the country their life had been one of grim and incessant conflict with all manner of difficulties. Not only were they met again and again by the deadly hostility and persecution of the North-West Fur Company, who were determined to destroy the colony brought out under the care of their rivals in trade; not only had locust plagues and epidemics assailed them with ruinous force, but the very elements seemed so unfriendly to people unaccustomed to the climatic conditions, that more than ten long years from their first coming had passed before they had any means of livelihood other than the fish or fowl or products of the chase they might ofttimes with great hardship and suffering secure. Even following those ten years they had scarcely got their homes built and their little plots sowed, when, after the "long and cruel winter" of 1826, the raging Red swept everything they owned before its frothing current into Lake Winnipeg. Is it any wonder that when they got fairly settled, the old men who had come through this magnificent struggle felt that now when their sinews had been tamed by age and trouble and their heads frosted with the unmelting snows, they were entitled to that decade of rest that rounds out the threescore years and ten?

And so it was that the older of them, while loyal to every British institution that might be set up in their midst, and while anxious to do what was best for their children, waited in the lengthening shadows for the sunset, and neither clamored for changed conditions nor took much active part in them when those conditions began to obtain. The younger people amongst them, it is true—many of whom, as I have said in my former volume, had gone to eastern institutions of learning and had come back with some knowledge of life's possibilities under different conditions; and others of whom had, in freighting expeditions, tapped the arteries of business and got the taste of commercial blood—were not averse to the incoming of the new life when circumstances would be ripe for its advent.

The other part of the community was composed largely of the *bois-brulès*—the adventurous hunters and traders of the time—and these could have no special interest in pressing for the opening of the country to the newer civilization. From their childhood these men had roamed over this great area with a lordly sense of ownership. Without any let or hindrance they had followed the buffalo over the trackless prairie; they had trapped the fur-bearing animals in the forest and on the plains; they had fished in the great lakes and rivers, and in the midst of it all had lived in the enjoyment of a satisfying, if rude, abundance. No one who ever saw one of these plain hunters come in to Fort Garry after the season's work on the Saskatchewan, could fail to see that he was a person in exceedingly comfortable material circumstances. In his train he had any number of carts (with ponies for each and to spare), and these were laden with the choicest viands in the shape of buffalo meat, marrow fat, beaver-tail, etc., while he also had a goodly supply of furs that would bring handsome prices. Besides his ponies, he had several choice horses of the larger breed for buffalo runners; and camping with his family and following in their cosy tents on the prairie, he was as independent as a feudal baron in the brave days of old. Under such circumstances these men were not likely to be active in securing the advent of conditions that would circumscribe their domain; but neither they nor any other class of the population were predisposed to put obstacles in the way of any incoming system that would pay due regard to the rights of those who were in the country before its advent.

Summing up the whole situation, then, it would seem that things had to take their normal course, and that circumstances were shaping so that in the fulness of time the West was to come to its majority and clothe itself in the garments of national citizenship. The number of people from the eastern provinces who began looking westward, and the increase of publications concerning the country by those visiting it, directed the attention of statesmen to its great possibilities, and prepared the way for the movement that secured the "Great Lone Land" as a part of the Dominion of Canada.

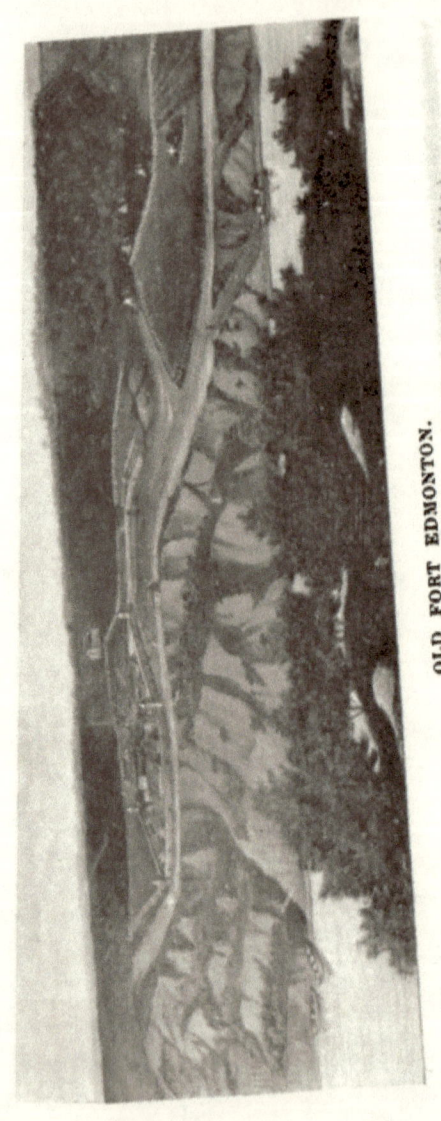

OLD FORT EDMONTON.

(From family of the late Senator Hardisty.)

CHAPTER II.

PATHOS AND PERILS OF CHANGE.

There is always a strong element of pathos in the way in which the people who have been in undisputed and absolute possession of a country, realize that limitations are being put upon them by the incoming of new population and new conditions. A few years ago it was my privilege to be present on an island in one of our western lakes when the Indians of the district were assembled for the annual treaty payment and the usual supply of rations. Everyone knows how fairly and honorably the Indians of the West have been treated by the Government, and, for the most part, by their agents, and we all realize how the progress of the world and the good of mankind necessitate the acquisition of the land from those who have not had the training or the opportunity required to fully develop its resources; but, withal, the scene at one of these

Indian treaties has its sadness for the thoughtful onlooker. As the men who had once been lords of the isles and lakes sat meekly round in a circle to receive each his handful of flour and piece of bacon for the mid-day meal, one could not help feeling that our duty as a Christian people is not wholly done when we bestow a meal, pay a few dollars and provide a reservation. The children of the wild, upon whose heritage we have entered, must become the wards of the nation and the charge of the Church of Christ, that their declining days may be cheered and brightened in the noblest sense.

As one of an armed force I have witnessed the surrender of princely Crees and Chippewyans beyond the banks of the North Saskatchewan—many of them men of magnificent mould and royal bearing—who had been incited to rebellion by people who should have known better. When these misguided men laid down their arms and were guarded by our wakeful pickets, thoughts of pity for their unhappy predicament filled the minds of their guards in the watches of the night. These Indians must be taught by force, if need be, the wrong of rebellion against a rightly constituted authority that is disposed to treat them fairly; and above all, they must be taught the sacredness of human life. But seeing that in the interests of progressive civilization we have policed the plains over which they once roamed as "monarchs of all they surveyed," that we have placed limitations upon them to which they were wholly unaccustomed, and which were not provided for in their own dark code of ethics, we ought to be more ready to follow them with the blessings of peace than with the waste of the sword.

These somewhat extreme examples will serve to illustrate our opening sentence as to the element of pathos present when people who have had illimitable range begin to find themselves circumscribed, even though this narrowing of the field is for their own ultimate good. They give us to understand how the white settlers by the banks of the Red and Assiniboine rivers, though perfectly ready to acquiesce in the new order of things beginning to obtain amongst them, would feel that a great change was coming over the spirit of their dream. Those who know what the old order had been realize how completely in many ways it was to be reversed, and hence how carefully and judiciously the Government of Canada, and those who professed to be its agents, should have acted in bringing the change to pass. For those settlers, once they had conquered their earlier difficulties, life had been singularly peaceable and uneventful. Its central points outside the home, with all its guileless hospitality and simplicity, were the church and school, both of which bulked far more largely with them than some people in these days of complex society seem able to understand.

They were without the vexation and the heart-burning of active politics, they were ignorant of taxation in any form, while the rivalries that existed were in keeping with their simple life, and had nothing of that fierce element of competition into which the newer civilization was to hurl them. The contests that had been most in evidence were over such matters as the speed of horses, in regard to which the settlement would often be deeply stirred, especially if the horses were owned in different parts of the colony. There was sometimes a great deal of strength put into efforts to be first with the seeding, harvest, hay-cutting, hay-hauling or freighting expeditions. It was the ambition of many households always to have breakfast by candle-light, that they might have a good deal done before their more tardy neighbors arose. In the matter of hay-hauling we used to get up in the night, and going out to the yard, where the oxen had been tied to the carts, grope round in the darkness to get them hitched up, now and then pausing to listen whether we could hear the creaking music that betokened the departure of our neighbor's cart-train to the hay swamps. Friendly contests in feats of physical strength were very common. The number of bags of wheat a man could carry on his back, the quantity of shot-bags he could lift over his head, the weight he could hang to his little finger and then write his name on the wall with a coal, the number of loads of hay he could cut with a scythe in a day, or the number of "stooks" of wheat he could handle with a sickle—these were some of the rivalries that gave zest to the simple life of the early days. The school was another field for competition, and on the great days of oral examination the parents and friends were present as eager and interested spectators of the contest which decided who was the best reader, writer, etc., in the district.

In the business life of the people there was nothing tumultuous. There were no banks and no promissory notes—on the latter of which they would have looked with contempt as on something implying distrust in a man's word of honor. The general stores, either of the

Hudson's Bay Company or of individual dealers, were not clamorous for business, as there was no compelling force of competition. Frequently on going to one of these stores you had to look up the proprietor, who, leaving the store to take care of itself, was out attending to his horse, or something of that sort. When you went into a store there was no modern clerk to advance with an alluring smile; indeed, the proprietor or clerk might even say that he had not the article asked for, until the customer would wander round and find it for himself. No wrapping paper was used, and you had either to bring a bag with you, buy some cotton, or leave your tea and sugar on the counter.

Think of a community like that being suddenly confronted with the necessity for political strife, with the prospect of municipal government and taxation, with all the keen and sometimes bitter rivalries of present-day business methods, and with, alas, some adventurers all too ready to take advantage of their simple-heartedness, and no one will wonder if it took the people some little time to gather themselves up and accommodate their lives to such new conditions.

But more important in its bearing upon the feeling of the people was the sudden realization of the fact that, after long years of undisputed possession of large privileges on the great areas around them, limitations were being put upon their operations by the incoming of strangers, who, driving stakes here and there, barred the old ways and the old fields—sometimes unjustly —against a people who could only be expected to learn slowly that their domain must some time be curtailed. There was an element of pathos, and yet, withal, of sound reason in all this, in view of which those who were bringing in the new conditions would have done well to exercise a caution and care they did not always manifest. Add to this the fact that ofttimes it was discovered that the persons who, by show of authority, sometimes excluded the settlers from places, had themselves no rightful claim, and one should not be surprised if the settlers under such circumstances were in some unrest as to the future. I remember, for instance, how the hay meadows to which the settlers had come for many years, with the marking out of a "circle" as the only condition precedent to holding all within it, were closed against them by people who, coming from the village around Fort Garry, desired to hold these meadows for their own profit. If they had just claim it was all right, but if they had not their action was resented. The settlers, however, were not slow to seize the situation, and some incidents took place which showed, to the disgust of the discomfited, that they could hold their own. The "green knoll swamp," lying between the Kildonan settlers and Stony Mountain, was a favorite source of hay supply, and new-comers, finding this out, often came round with formidable papers to frighten the settlers away from their accustomed haunts. A friend of mine still relates with great relish that one day, just as he and the people of his immediate neighborhood were starting into hay-cutting there, an important-looking stranger with a large retinue of men, mowers, rakes, etc., bore down upon him, and with book in hand asked him in great wrath who the people were who dared to come upon this land, as he wished to have them arrested for trespass. The settler, standing upon his mower, told him that the Gunns, McDonalds, MacBeths, Pritchards, Harpers and Sutherlands were visible. All these names were taken down with tremendous emphasis by the irate gentleman, who expected that the settler would at once warn his neighbors, and that he and they would "fold their tents like the Arabs, and silently steal away" from the coveted hay-fields. In this, however, the new-comer was mistaken, for the settler coolly went on to say,

"You have not yet taken me down in your book. My name is Francis Murray," upon which the man "with curses not loud but deep," seeing that his game was understood, took himself away and was not again heard from.

Besides all this, some of the new arrivals, who had been hospitably entertained by the settlers with their best, wrote to eastern papers ridiculing the manner of life and the accommodation they found amongst them, and made reference to the dark-skinned people under the somewhat contemptuous name of "breeds." The number, of course, who did any of these things was small, but their conduct offended and estranged many who, ignorant of the fact that such people were only the excrescences on the better life of the older provinces, somewhat guardedly awaited further developments.

In the meantime matters were shaping in the direction of a confederation in Canada,—and when that movement, beginning in the Maritime districts, had spread westward, the great statesmen of all parties, dropping their minor differences, united nobly in accomplishing it, so that in the year 1867 the older provinces came together into one federation with provincial autonomy in regard to certain matters. This task once finished it would seem as if Canadian statesmen looked round for fresh worlds to conquer, and as the great West was beginning to attract attention, steps were taken in the Dominion Parliament to secure through the Imperial Government the surrender by the Hudson's Bay Company of their charter in Rupert's Land. This charter they had held for some three hundred years, and they naturally declined to give it up without compensation for the loss they would sustain by relinquishing claim to the vast territory it covered. Instructed by the Dominion Government, Sir George E. Cartier and the Hon. William Macdougall proceeded to England, and arrangements were concluded for the transfer of the North-West to Canada. The Hudson's Bay Company were to receive £300,000 sterling, certain reservations around their posts, and about one-twentieth of the lands in the territory as thereafter surveyed, and were therefor to surrender their charter to the Imperial Government; the latter were to transfer the territory to the Government of Canada, who in their turn undertook to respect and conserve the rights of the people in the area thus added to the Dominion. This arrangement was concluded in the spring of 1869, and it was then expected that the purchase money would be paid on

the 1st of October following, and that probably
on the 1st day of December the Queen's
Proclamation would issue, setting forth these
facts and fixing the date of the actual transfer
of the North-West to Canada.

So far all was well. The ideas leading to the
acquisition of this great territory were in every
sense statesmanlike, and if carefully carried out
were calculated to be of the greatest benefit to
the people in the new territory and to the
Dominion as well. We cannot too thankfully
pay tribute unstinted to the men whose ideals
were for an ever-widening horizon, and who felt
that "no pent-up Utica should confine the
powers" of the young nation just beginning to
stretch out and exercise its giant limbs. Once
the older provinces were brought into a
Confederation it was wise to look forward to a
Canada extending from ocean to ocean, and to
take the necessary legal steps to secure the
West as part of the Dominion. But just there,
after the negotiations with the Hudson's Bay
Company through the Imperial Government
were well in hand and were being wisely concluded, the Canadian authorities seem to have
blundered by overlooking the fact that the new
territory had a population of some ten thousand
people, who ought at least to have been

informed in some official way of the bargain that was being made, and of the steps being taken to secure and guard their rights and privileges.

Rumors of the transaction certainly reached the Red River through unauthoritative sources, only to produce uneasiness there. Before the transfer was completed men were sent out to open roads from the Lake of the Woods into the settlement. Surveying parties entered the new territory and went hither and thither, driving their stakes and erecting their mounds, to the bewilderment of the people, and, to cap all, a governor was despatched to the Red River before the old Government was in any sense superseded and before a Queen's Proclamation, which would have been instantly recognized by all classes of the community, was issued. The Selkirk settlers and other people of that class, however perplexed at the procedure, had the utmost confidence that the Canadian authorities would ultimately do substantial justice in the recognition of all just and lawful claims and privileges enjoyed by the inhabitants of the new territory, and hence awaited patiently, though somewhat anxiously, the developments of time. But the French half-breeds (commonly called "the French" in the Red River Colony)—more fiery and easily excited, more turbulent of spirit and warlike in disposition, accustomed to passages at arms with any who would cross their path, and withal, as a class, less well-informed on current events than their white brethren— were not satisfied with a course that seemed to them to place their rights in jeopardy, and so they rose up in a revolt that, alas, while possibly accomplishing some of the objects which should have been reached by constitutional means, left its red stream across the page of our history.

CHAPTER III.

ARMED REBELLION.

"THE French are off to drive back the Governor!" These words, somewhat excitedly uttered by one of my brothers, and addressed to my father, made up the first intimation I, a lad of ten summers, had that something serious was on foot; yet I recall the exact words as distinctly as if they had been spoken yesterday, and most of the acts in the drama of the rebellion whose actual outbreak they announced are indelibly stamped upon my memory. It was in October, 1869, and my brother had just come home from the morning service in Kildonan church, over which upon that day the shadow of the situation had been cast, perhaps to the serious detriment of devout and undivided worship. The fact that the news first came to us in this way throws a curious side-light on the primitive life of the time. The churchyard was the modern representative of the Athenian market-place, so far as the giving and receiving of news was concerned. The settlement had no telegraphic communication with the outside world; the solitary post-office was miles away, and mails, in any case, were few and far apart. A few of the people subscribed for an eastern paper, which was comparatively old before it reached its destination, and the local paper was doubtless often greatly at a loss for "copy." Moreover, it must be remembered that in certain seasons of the year the settlers were away from home haying, wood-cutting, etc., during the whole week. Saturday evening, however, they were all back. A general brushing-up was in order, and on Sabbath morning, except in cases of sickness or some similar cause, they were all wending their way in good time to the church.

"What's the latest news?" was a question requently heard, and the men often gathered in knots in the churchyard before the service that they might get abreast of the times. Some stay-at-home man, perhaps the school-teacher, who was always looked upon as a species of encyclopædia, or someone who was in touch with the inhabitants of Fort Garry, "held the floor," and gave what information he could as to current events. The Sabbatarian ideas of these people were, for the most part, strict enough; but I suppose they looked on this parliament as a sort of family gathering to talk over family affairs, and as a general thing the news imparted was not startling enough to disturb that air of devoutness which they sought to cultivate when they entered the portals of the place of worship. But on the day just mentioned the intelligence was of unusual moment, and, perchance, may have deepened the earnestness with which they joined in the prayer for the preservation of peace to Him " who breaketh the bow in sunder and burneth the chariot in the fire."

"The French are off to drive back the Governor!" repeated my brother, fresh from the churchyard conclave, and though it was the first I recall hearing of active trouble, doubtless the announcement was not wholly unexpected by my father. It seemed that for some weeks previous to this Louis Riel, who was to have the "bad eminence" of leading two rebellions, had been holding meetings amongst the French half-breeds, and, doubtless, moved by others far and near, had been delivering fiery orations in regard to the rumored changes which he claimed were to put in jeopardy all the rights they held dear. It may as well be admitted that the situation, as they saw it, gave him some plausible ground on which to work. The difficulty of conveying reliable information from the outside world to the settlement must not be overlooked; but we repeat that it now seems passing strange that the Government of Canada did not in some way get official word to the

LOUIS RIEL.

settlers before sending forward a governor, and letting loose in the territory some not overprudent persons who claimed to be the agents of the Dominion. Had some man as widely known and respected in the country as Donald A. Smith, who, coming afterwards, even when the revolt was at white heat, did so much to secure peace—had such a man been sent at that stage, the face of our history might have been changed.

But these are large provisos; and, in the absence of any such precautions, the signal fires for rebellion were lit on the banks of the Red River, and called sympathizers from out on the great plains. Add to the situation as it was the fact that Riel had commanding influence over those French half-breeds, and we find additional explanation for the uprising. His father, who lived many years in St. Boniface, and was sometimes called "the Miller of the Seine," from his having a mill on that little tributary to the Red, had been an idolized leader amongst them, and the son inherited much of his immense energy and eloquence. Moreover, it must be remembered that Riel's fiery speeches fell upon very inflammable material. These men were naturally of stormy spirit—daring rough-riders of the plains, who brooked no interference from anyone, and who had passed through many a conflict with their darker brethren on the wild wastes of the West. Once get men of that sort to feel that they are fighting for their homes and the rights of their families, put modern weapons into their hands, and in their own kind of warfare they are dangerous men to attack. Being of that stamp, and being made to feel that they were to be trodden upon, they rose in armed insurrection; and, as a first step, went on the errand noted in the opening words of this chapter. No one can defend an act such as theirs, even had it not led to some of the deplorable events which followed. Though many can see extenuating circumstances, armed rebellion is a serious business; and if there is a place for it in the present state of the world, it is when all constitutional means have been exhausted, and people accomplish a revolution in the face of some iniquitous and tyrannous government. Tubal Cain's offensive weapon is an instrument of last resort, only to be taken up when every other arbitrament has failed; and this we say, though we agree

> " That while Oppression lifts its head,
> Or a tyrant would be lord,
> While we may thank him for the plough,
> We won't forget the sword."

But the case before us was far short of that. At best Riel and his men were starting to fight the shadows of events which might never come, even though those shadows seemed to their kindled imaginations to be portents of dire disasters heading in their direction. No threat had been made against these people, and they should have known that no act of robbery or of deprivation of rights had ever been permitted ultimately by the flag under whose folds they were to be governed. Besides, they had no right to assume to speak for the whole country before consulting with others who lived in it. Why did they not take counsel with the Selkirk settlers and men of that class who, being of less nomadic habits, had larger settled interests in the territory, and who, moreover, had always been better informed as to events that were transpiring ? Why did they not see whether some concerted and peaceful action on the part of the whole population could not be planned to attain the ends in view and conserve the rights of the inhabitants which seemed to be threatened ? And yet, though we ask these questions, we cannot be justly bitter towards the mass of the rebels at that stage. They were easily imposed upon and led by many who should have counselled peace, and notably by the ill-starred man who, twenty-five years afterwards, selfishly offered to give up the struggle for alleged popular rights in exchange for a sum of money for himself. Whether Louis Riel had all his senses or not God only knoweth, and now that he has gone beyond the bar of human judgment, we pronounce not whether in our opinion he was knave or lunatic, or partly both. We give some of the facts concerning him in the following pages, and let the reader bring in a verdict if he chooses so to do.

CHAPTER IV.

THE PLOT THICKENS.

THE first overt act of rebellion was committed when an armed and organized force, on the 21st of October, 1869, took possession of the highway near the Salle River, between Fort Garry and the international boundary. By this route the Hon. Wm. Macdougall and his staff would have entered the territory in the normal course of things, but the rebels put an effectual stop to the programme by interposing on the one great roadway an obstacle which the Governor's aide is reported as having somewhat irreverently designated "a blawsted fence." A fence extending only a few yards each way across a roadway in a prairie district that can be travelled in almost any direction need not necessarily prevent people from traversing the country, but this one erected upon that highway was in tangible form a declaration that the armed men who erected it had made up their minds to oppose the entrance of the new *régime* into the territory. At this primitive barricade a large body of men were camped, with horses at hand for service at any moment, and they let down or put up the bars according as they viewed with approval or otherwise the passing of any who came that way.

It was the regular travelled route of the freighters from the United States to Fort Garry, and the force at the fence examined all the cart and waggon trains. The commissariat had to be supplied, and while dry goods were allowed to pass without much detention, the articles of moister texture and of edible description were quite freely confiscated to the use of the camp. The mail-bags they also diligently examined in search of documents that might furnish plausible excuse for the uprising, and to prevent any communications with whose contents they were unacquainted reaching the friends of the new *régime* in the settlement. The new governor, of course, was the especial object of their search, and every equipage about which a governor could be concealed was scrutinized by them as keenly as the cars are explored by lynx-eyed trainmen in the season when tramps are stealing free rides across the country. One of the Kildonan settlers found this out one day, somewhat to his alarm, when he tried to play a harmless joke after the elephantine manner supposed to be characteristic of us Scotchmen. It appears that the settler was bringing in from St. Cloud a Presbyterian missionary who was coming out for the first time to take part in the church work of the West, and upon their arrival at the fence they were stopped and interrogated in the customary way. The missionary being a somewhat magisterial-looking man, it occurred to the settler that the obstructionists were eyeing him with considerable suspicion, and so thinking to have some diversion he waited for the question, " Whom have you here ?" " Our governor," he replied. The words were scarcely out of his mouth before there was such a " mustering in hot haste," and such a threatening display of fire-arms that the settler thought the joke had gone about far enough, and so, without much loss of time, said : " Perhaps I had better explain for fear we misunderstand each other. If you are looking for the new governor of the country I haven't got him, but this gentleman here is a governor in our church." After a little parley the settler, who was quite well known to some of the party, was allowed to pass through with the man of peace, the latter, perhaps, more thankful than ever before that he held a commission from higher authority than that of earthly potentates.

Every effort short of force was being used by the local authorities, the Governor of the Hudson's Bay Company, and his Council, to secure a peaceable solution of the difficulties impending, but to all these the rebels turned a deaf ear, and a few days after the erection of the barricade a mounted troop of them, under command of Ambroise Lepine, rode to the place where Governor Macdougall had come upon British territory, and warned him to leave before nine o'clock next morning. They returned the following day at eight to see this programme carried out, and the Governor, having no other recourse in the presence of arms than to obey, recrossed the boundary line to Pembina, in the State of Dakota.

A striking figure was this Ambroise Lepine, as I remember seeing him in Fort Garry in the heyday of his power (and even as I saw him at the market-place in Winnipeg a few days ago, unbroken by the weight of sixty years or more) —a man of magnificent physique, standing fully six feet three and built in splendid proportion, straight as an arrow, with hair of raven blackness, large aquiline nose and eyes of piercing brilliance; a man of prodigious strength, a skilled rough rider and, withal, a dangerous subject to meet in conflict. He had great influence amongst his compatriots, and by reason, doubtless, of his physical prowess and striking military appearance, soon obtained control of their armed movements. No excuse can be made for his

AMBROISE LEPINE.

complicity in some of the events that transpired later, but of all the leaders of the rebellion he was the only one who manifested anything like manliness after it was over, by refusing to stay abroad and by submitting to arrest, saying that the law could take its course with him seeing he had only done what he thought was his duty. Speaking of that arrest by anticipation, it is told that when the two men who were entrusted with the duty of executing the warrant went to his house in the night, Lepine took a look at them, and remarking that he could knock their heads together if he wished, nevertheless got ready and went unresistingly along with them.*

To revert to the barricade again, we are not surprised to find that, as winter was coming on, the rebels began to look around for more comfortable quarters, and that accordingly, on the 3rd of November, they rode down to Fort Garry, and in spite of the protest of the Hudson's Bay officer in charge, entered upon possession of it, with all its stores and abundant supplies. It is quite well known that some (amongst them certain old pensioners from regiments formerly in the country) had expressed opinion that such a movement as this would take place, and had offered to garrison the fort, but there being difference of mind upon the point, nothing was done. Riel accordingly entered without forcible opposition, and proceeded to make himself comfortable by utilizing the furniture intended for Governor Macdougall; and as the provision of the fort was ample, the rebel chief and his followers

---

* Lepine was tried and sentenced to death, but the sentence was commuted by Lord Dufferin to two years' imprisonment and permanent forfeiture of his civic rights.

wore fine linen, the best of cloth capots, silk-worked moccasins, etc., and fared sumptuously every day.

It has been fashionable, in some quarters, to accuse the Hudson's Bay Company of conniving at this seizure and at the rebellion generally, but the utter absurdity of assertions like these is apparent to anyone who thinks upon the subject. The company had parted with their control of the country, which indeed was, in the nature of things, getting beyond their domination. They had nothing to gain and everything to lose by having the whole territory in a state of unrest, to the serious detriment of their trade, and were certainly to suffer a loss that could not well be appraised, by having Riel and his following quartered upon them for nearly a year. Besides this, Governor McTavish, the head of the company in the country, on the 16th of November, in view of the fact that Riel had called a convention from all parts of the settlement, issued a proclamation denouncing in the strongest terms the insurrectionary movement, calling upon those engaged in it to disperse to their homes, and with all the weight of his authority asking the convention to employ, in any movement in which they might engage to secure their rights, only such means as were "lawful, constitutional, rational and safe." I remember, too, hearing my father, who visited Governor McTavish in his sick-room about this time, say that he never witnessed anything more pathetic than the way in which the Governor referred to the fact that the insurgents had hauled down the Union Jack and hoisted an ensign of their own device with *fleur-de-lis* and shamrock, and how he said, "As I saw, through my window, the hoisting of their rag on our old flagstaff, I almost choked with mortification and shame." Add to these things, also, the fact that Riel, in the general convention held in February, after his entry into Fort Garry, made, according to the report in his own paper, the *New Nation*, a most bitter attack upon the Hudson's Bay Company, saying, amongst other things, that instead of having the prefix "honorable" they should have the title "shameful,"—consider all this and the theory as to collusion between them becomes exceedingly chimerical.

One of the first acts of Riel was to issue, under duress, from the *Nor'-Wester* office, a circular addressed to the people of the country, asking them to a convention to consider the situation of affairs; but in regard to this and any later convention called, if we can judge from his conduct as reported in his own organ, it seems as if he wished to give the outside world the impression that all the people of the country were in sympathy with him, while at the same time he was determined to have his own way, whatever the others advised.

If it be asked how it was that the other inhabitants of the country did not rise up and put the rebellion down at that stage or later, various answers might be given in the presence of some abortive efforts made by certain well-meaning people so to do. It is quite safe to say that the white settlers, at first, never dreamed that the movement would be carried as far as it was eventually, and we are equally safe in asserting that the leaders of the movement themselves went far beyond their original intention as they became the more intoxicated with power and success. It must be borne in mind that to these settlers Canada was practically an unknown quantity, and that they looked upon the quarrel as not theirs to settle in view of the circumstances that brought it about.

In the report of Colonel Dennis, chief of the staff of surveyors, and Governor Macdougall's deputy in the new territory, the matter is put in concise and very intelligible shape. The

Colonel had gone along the Red River to raise a force to escort the new Governor in, and he gives the following as the general expression of feeling: "We (the English-speaking settlers) feel confidence in the future administration of the government of this country under Canadian rule; at the same time we have not been consulted in any way as a people on entering into the Dominion. The character of the new government has been settled in Canada without our being consulted. We are prepared to accept it respectfully, obey the laws and become good subjects; but when you present to us the issue of a conflict with the French party, with whom we have hitherto lived in friendship, backed up as they would be by the Roman Catholic Church (which seems probable by the course taken by the priests), in which conflict it is almost certain the aid of the Indians would be invoked, and perhaps obtained by that party, we feel disinclined to enter upon it, and think *that the Dominion should assume the responsibility of establishing amongst us what it and it alone has decided upon.*"

Who is there whose calm common-sense will not say that this position was a reasonable one to take? As to the references made in the statement, that concerning the part taken by the priests had ground in the fact that the blockading party at the Salle River were quartered in part at Père Richot's house, that seditious meetings had been held on Sundays almost, if not altogether, in connection with the church services, and that O'Donoghue, perhaps the deepest and most dangerous of all the rebel leaders, was studying for the priesthood in St. Boniface. The reference to the probability of Indian aid being invoked and obtained is shown to have been reasonable by the fact that such aid was invoked and obtained with terrible effect under much less favorable circumstances, and against heavier odds, by practically the same parties, some fifteen years later, in the second rebellion.

So much in explanation of the position taken by the settlers other than the French at the outset. Later on, when the temper and attitude of Riel and his followers were such as to estrange from them any sympathy they might otherwise have had, the settlement was utterly unable to make any successful move against them, however much the people may have desired so to do. The rebels held a stone-walled and bastioned fort, built for defence; they held all the military stores of the country in Enfield rifles and cannon, and, as the *New Nation* said in one of its

February numbers, they had all the powder in the territory except a small and damaged lot at Lower Fort Garry. With all the Hudson's Bay stores in their power, a siege against the rebels would have been hopeless, even though the settlers could have left their homes in the dead of winter and camped around the fort, while to have attempted an assault with shotguns and scant ammunition would have been absurd.

As an example of the kind of arms some of the loyalist settlers were provided with, I myself saw more than one man at the rendezvous afterwards in Kildonan armed only with a bludgeon weighted with lead. We give due credit for good intention and even for valor to those who carried them, but to suggest an attack upon a fully-garrisoned fort such as we remember Fort Garry to have been at the time, with such weapons, was certainly giving small evidence of possessing that discretion which is valor's better part. And yet there were attempts made against the rebels, as we have already implied, but although the men who engaged in them doubtless meant well, it has scarcely required the after-light of twenty-five years to show that these attempts did more harm than good. They certainly led to the death of two excellent young men

—the one of the older, the other of the newer settlers—and to the intense suffering of many more; to the exasperation of the whole situation, and to the creation of a race and creed cleavage from which we have not yet wholly recovered.

There had been a time when a large portion of the French population did not follow Riel in his resort to arms, though they, in common with nearly all the people of the country, felt somewhat keenly anxious as to their rights under the incoming Government. On looking up records I find that my father, then a magistrate and a member of the Council of Assiniboia (the governing body in Hudson's Bay Company days), seconded, with the Hon. A. G. B. Bannatyne as mover, the following resolution: "That Messrs. Dease and Goulet be appointed to collect as many of the more respectable of the French community as possible, and with them proceed to the camp of the party who intend to intercept Hon. Mr. Macdougall, and endeavor to procure their peaceable dispersion." That the men sent failed in their mission does not disprove the fact that they had large loyal support amongst their own people. Moreover, we find that after Riel had seized Fort Garry he was at one time on the point of consenting to the Hudson's Bay Company continuing in authority till a committee of French and English could treat with Mr. Macdougall or with the Dominion direct, when a rumor that the Canadians around were about to move on Fort Garry put an end to the matter.

HON. A. G. B. BANNATYNE.

Besides all this, there was a time, even after the rebellion had gone some length, when, through the intervention of Mr. Bannatyne, three well-known French half-breeds, Francois Nolin, Augustin Nolin, and one Perreault, agreed to have a meeting of English and French to discuss their rights and send a statement of these to

Mr. Macdougall, whom, if he granted them, they would bring into the country in spite of Riel. It is said on good authority that these men with others were actually in council on the matter when a report reached them that the Canadians, together with the English-speaking settlers, were combining to attack the French. This seemed to the friendly half-breeds to mean that the French element was to be coerced without regard to their rights, and hence, though some of the French half-breeds never joined Riel, the opposition offered by these movements against him practically solidified the great body of them in sympathy with his position, and led to serious consequences.

These movements, however, though in some cases irresponsibly organized, were doubtless entered upon with the best intention on the part of those engaged in them, and we shall give a few reminiscent sketches of them in the next chapter.

CHAPTER V.

SOME COUNTER-EFFORTS AND THEIR RESULTS.

LARGE "ifs" always stand stiffly in the way, and therefore we gain little now by saying that if the Hon. William Macdougall had returned to Ottawa, instead of remaining on the frontier, and if his deputies and agents within the new territory had been more discreet, we might have been spared some of the deplorable scenes that followed. The Governor on the frontier was an irritant to the rebels, and the agents or alleged agents within were a ferment in the midst of the elements composing the population. Both parties were doubtless actuated by the very best motives and most loyal intentions, but the retirement of the one and the silence of the other would have left the incensed and (in their own view) wronged rebels without any excuse for openly assailing the residents of the community and depriving some of their liberty and others, alas, of their lives. The

Governor was ill-advised by friends in the territory, "on no account to leave Pembina," and by communication between them the unreasonable idea of some forcible effort to put down the rebellion was kept alive, with the irritating results already noticed. On the 1st day of December it was expected that the new territory would have been formally transferred to Canada, and so upon that day Governor Macdougall issued what purported to be a Queen's Proclamation appointing him as Governor of the territory, and another proclamation, signed by himself as Governor, appointing Col. Dennis his Deputy within the territory, with power to raise and equip a force wherewith to overcome the rebellious element. No one feels disposed to impugn Mr. Macdougall's good faith and good intention in taking this course, but it turned out to have been taken without due authority, and for the unwarrantable use made of the Queen's name he was severely censured by the Canadian Government.

When it was discovered that what was called the Queen's Proclamation was not so in reality, the situation became more chaotic than ever : but in the meantime Col. Dennis thought he was justified in raising an armed force to overturn the rebel power, and with the aid of others proceeded so to do. One of the first results was the gathering of some forty-five men in the house of Dr. Schultz, in the village near Fort Garry, to protect some Government supplies; but this handful was practically nothing against the rebel force in Fort Garry. Accordingly, when, a few days later, a force of some three hundred rebels, well armed and with several pieces of artillery, came towards the flimsy building, the poorly equipped little garrison did the only sensible thing under the circumstances and surrendered without resistance. They were disarmed and imprisoned in Fort Garry, some, amongst them Schultz himself, being placed in solitary confinement.

Schultz was a man his captors feared with a wholesome dread. For a number of years he had been active in the affairs of the country, especially in connection with the agitation for free trade and for closer connection with the Empire, and was known as a man very impatient of restraint and in many ways difficult to handle. Physically he was of giant stature and possessed of almost incredible strength, as some who attempted his arrest in connection with the free-trade and other squabbles in the country had found to their cost. I remember when a boy running beside him, as with powerful stride he walked from our home to the river on an occasion when I was sent to direct him to a house which he was to visit on a medical consultation, and I can yet see the oars bending like willows in his strong hands as he propelled the rough boat against the waves. I recall, too, hearing how once at a meeting in the town a riot was feared, and how Schultz, who was seated on a great home-made oaken chair, rose, and putting his foot on one of the bars, wrenched the chair asunder as if it had been made of pipestems, after seeing which the crowd decided that if they were going to do any rioting they would leave him unmolested at any rate. A man of that physical stamp and, withal, of somewhat inflammatory cast of mind, the rebels thought they had better keep apart and well guarded; hence they placed him alone, and, as afterwards appeared, they fully intended to put a sudden end to his career.

But they were to be baulked of their prey. Certain delicacies from friends were allowed him, and it is said that in a pudding one day a knife and a gimlet were concealed. With the knife he cut into strips the buffalo robe he slept upon and such clothing as he could spare, and having with the aid of the gimlet fastened the line thus made to the wall, he let himself out of the window on the night of the 23rd of January. His ponderous weight was too much for the slender rope, and while yet quite a distance from the ground the line broke and the escaping prisoner came to the earth with great force, injuring his leg somewhat seriously. A less determined man would have given up, as there was still the high stone wall to scale, but in some way he managed it and in due time was on the outside of the fort. The night was dark and stormy, with cold wind and whirling snow, and Schultz, somewhat dazed by the fall, missed his bearings, only realizing his whereabouts when he came on landmarks which told him he was making for St. Boniface. That was not very satisfactory, so he turned and nearly ran up against a sentry at one of the fort gates! But by this he had found his latitude and as rapidly as he could walk and run he made his way to my father's house in Kildonan, about six miles away from the place of his captivity.

I have heard it said on good authority lately (though I have no personal knowledge of the fact), that up to that time the relations subsisting between Schultz and my father were not the most cordial, perhaps because the former was bitterly opposed to the Hudson's Bay Company, while my father would not allow anything said against the Company in his presence. If any such coldness did exist between them previous to that night, the coming of Schultz for refuge to my father's house was but another instance of that shrewd, far-sighted knowledge of human nature for which he was always noted. Apart altogether from my father's well-known contempt for the alleged government of Riel, he was too much of a Highlander to close his door against even an enemy when he was wearied and hard-hunted, or else he would have been unworthy of the name that has become synonymous with hospitality, and has been immortalized by Scott in the famous meeting of Fitz-James and Roderick Dhu.

I remember well the arrival of Schultz at our house. It was in the grey dawn, and a cold morning at that, when a knocking came at the door, which my father rose and opened. I can recall his surprised exclamation, "Bless me, doctor, is this really you?" Then I can see the fugitive enter, thinly clad, tall, haggard and gaunt, and as soon as he had assured himself that there were no servants in the house who might betray him, he told the story of his escape as we have just related it. My father escorted his guest upstairs, watched over him while he slept, and all that afternoon the two remained there, conversing only in whispers so that their voices would not be heard by any who might come into the house. Again and again that day Riel's scouts, on their red-blanketed horses, passed by the door looking for their escaped prisoner, concerning whom Riel said to the Rev. George Young, "The guards are out looking for him, and they have orders to shoot him on sight."

Meanwhile my brother Alexander had gone into town and secured from his friends a pair or two of pistols, which were duly brought and handed upstairs, where a new programme was made out. Schultz was determined that he would never be taken alive, hence he decided that if the scouts entered the house he would sell his life as dearly as possible and neither give nor take quarter. For two days he remained there, and on the second night my father's favorite horse, "Barney," was hitched up, and the brother above mentioned drove the hunted man, by an unfrequented road, to the Indian settlement near Selkirk, whence, accompanied by the faithful Joseph Monkman, he made that terrible mid-winter journey on foot to eastern Canada. Afterwards we heard that some of the scouts had located him when in our house, but that either out of respect to my father, who had doubtless befriended many of them, or from dread of the desperate man they were hunting, they concluded not to enter.

In after years when I heard Sir John Schultz say that he "had still the shattered remnants of a good constitution," I used to account for the "shattering" by thinking of the desperate leap from the prison, the running with maimed limb and scanty clothing six miles in an arctic atmosphere, and then the fearful journey on foot across the rocky shores and wind-swept bays of Lake Superior to the cities of the East. Whether he and my father were warm friends before or not, they certainly were after that experience in the "City of Refuge;" and born orator as Sir John was, he never made a more graceful allusion in spoken words than he did when, at the unveiling of the Seven Oaks monument, he spoke of the man who at great personal risk opened the door of welcome to him in his extremity.

Meanwhile, the other prisoners were detained in Fort Garry, Riel was taking steps to form a provisional government, and Mr. Donald A. Smith (now Lord Strathcona and Mount Royal) had arrived from the East as a special com-

missioner from the Dominion Government to
settle the existing difficulties. By reason of his
long experience in the country and the great
respect in which he was held by all classes, Mr.
Smith's arrival was hailed with pleasure. Ex-
ercising rare skill and tact, he secured from Riel
the calling of an assemblage of all the settlers
on the 19th of January, for the purpose of hearing the commission read as to the purpose and
scope of Mr. Smith's mission. About ten days
before this Riel had caused to be published the
slate of the so-called Provisional Government,
the principal part of which consisted in the
declaration of himself as President, O'Donoghue
as Secretary-Treasurer, and Ambroise Lepine as
Adjutant-General.

Many racy incidents are related by those
who were present at the Assembly on the 19th
of January to hear Mr. Smith's commission.
Probably a thousand or more had gathered,
so the meeting had to be held in the open
air. An open-air meeting with the ther-
mometer over twenty degrees below zero
could hardly be called a deliberative assembly,
as the conditions were not favorable to ab-
sorption in the subject. Mr. Smith is said
to have refused to read his papers under the
hybrid ensign of the rebel government, and so

the Union Jack had to be displayed. Then Riel, who was becoming more and more of a "megalomaniac," wished to prevent the papers being read at all, on which a well-known settler caught the redoubtable President by the back of the collar and pulled him down the steps on which he was standing. Riel immediately threw off his coat (which in falling struck my father, to whom Riel, true to his French politeness, even in his rage, said "*Pardon, monsieur*"), and called out the guard. The gates were closed and things generally looked ugly, but finally quiet was restored and the papers read. At the close of the reading, on motion of Riel himself, seconded by Mr. A. G. B. Bannatyne, it was resolved that a convention consisting of twenty men from the English and twenty from the French side be called for the 25th of January to consider the whole matter of Mr. Smith's mission, and to formulate such a programme as seemed best for the country.

This meeting on the 19th January was the first direct blow given to Riel's position; or, changing the figure, it was the first real undermining of his authority, and Mr. Smith, as Commissioner from a Government which now showed every anxiety to do what was fair to all classes, scored a most decided and influential victory. One cannot help feeling now that had counter-movements against Riel (which could not possibly succeed under the circumstances) ceased, there would have been a bloodless settlement of the whole business; but the irritation caused by military movements against him, coupled with the fact that his star was on the wane, led doubtless to the horrible murder he shortly afterwards committed in the vain hope of establishing his authority beyond dispute.

The convention of forty French and English representatives met as called on the 25th of January, and continued from day to day till the 11th of February. The best existing report of that convention is found in the *New Nation*, Riel's organ, which is in the possession of Mr. J. P. Robertson, in the Provincial Library of Manitoba. The file, which was purchased from Mr. Wm. Coldwell, the ablest newspaper man of his time, tells an eloquent tale even in its appearance. The first page of it is called *The Red River Pioneer*, Vol. I., No. I.; the next page is blank, and on the following one we read, *The New Nation*, Vol. I., No. I. The explanation is that Mr. Coldwell was just beginning the publication of the *Pioneer* when Riel came down upon him, and *vi et armis* nipped it in the bud and established with its plant the *New Nation*, under control of one of his own following. Whoever reported the proceedings of the Convention of Forty for the *New Nation* did it well, not only as wielding a facile pen, but wielding it impartially, since several things not at all flattering to Riel are preserved. We have, too, the record of some hot passages-at-arms in which Riel was distinctly worsted.

The chairman of the convention was Judge Black, head of the law courts in the territory, a man of commanding intellect, of great forensic ability, and such noble bent of character that he had the utmost confidence of the whole community. During the convention we find he made several speeches of considerable length, in which occur passages of lofty and impassioned eloquence. Next to Judge Black, whose official position gave him prominence, the most influential and distinctively directing spirit was James Ross, a man of singular ability, deep learning and rare fluency of utterance. He was a son of Sheriff Ross, who had been famous as a leading man and an historian in the early days of the country. James Ross, who was a native of Red River, had graduated with high honors from Toronto University, had been a leading writer on the *Globe* there, and was an able lawyer. Despite the slanders of adventurers, he is remembered as one who had at heart the highest good of the country in which he was born. His legal accomplishments and intimate knowledge of the Canadian constitution made

JAMES ROSS.

him a most indispensable member of the convention, and to his opinions the greatest deference was paid. Amongst the other members were several who afterwards became prominent in the history of the country, and who even then showed remarkable acquaintance with public questions.

This convention was of great importance, and

hence the full list of members selected for it is here given, with the sections of the country they represented.

French Representatives.

St. Paul's—
  Pierre Thibert.
  Alex. Pagé.
  Magnus Birston.

St. Francois Xavier—
  Xavier Pagé
  Pierre Poitras.

St. Charles—
  Baptiste Beauchemin.

St. Vital—
  Louis Riel.
  Andrè Beauchemin.

Point Coupee—
  Louis Lacerte.
  Pierre Delorme.

St. Norbert—
  Pierre Paranteau.
  Norbert Laronce.
  B. Touton.

St. Boniface—
  W. B. O'Donoghue.
  Ambroise Lepine.
  Joseph Genton.
  Louis Schmidt.

Oak Point—
  Thomas Harrison.
  Charles Nolin.

Point à Grouette
  George Klyne.

English Representatives.

St. Peter's—
  Rev. Henry Cochrane.
  Thomas Spence.

St. Clement's—
  Thomas Bunn.
  Alex. McKenzie.

Kildonan—
  John Fraser.
  John Sutherland.

St. James'—
  George Flett.
  Robert Tait.

Some Counter-Efforts and Their Results. 69

St. Andrew's —
   Judge Black.
   Donald Gunn, sen.
   Alfred Boyd.

St. Paul's—
   Dr. C. J. Bird.

St. John's—
   James Ross.

St. Mary's—
   Kenneth McKenzie.

Headingly—
   John Taylor.
   Wm. Londsdale.

St. Margaret's—
   Wm. Cummings.

St. Anne's—
   George Gunn.
   D. Spence.

Winnipeg—
   Alfred H. Scott.

As there are some people even to this day who claim that Riel was loyal to British interests, though anxious about the privileges and rights of his countrymen, it may be worth while to give a few extracts from the report in his own paper: "For my part I would like to see the power of Canada limited in this country; that's what I want." "England chose to neglect us for one or two centuries back, and I do not suppose we are under any very great obligations to keep her laws." "For my part I do not want to be more British than I can help."

Amongst the incidents of the convention we notice in the report an attempt on the part of Riel to rebuke Mr. John (afterwards Senator) Sutherland, of Kildonan, who hotly replied that he had been giving his time all winter without fee or reward to efforts for the good of the country, that he was there to speak for the people who sent him, and did not propose to be taught his duty by Louis Riel. At another point three of the French half-breed representatives, Nolin, Klyne and Harrison, incurred the displeasure of Riel by voting against a motion

SENATOR SUTHERLAND.

he had submitted suggesting that the Hudson's Bay Company be ignored in all bargains made as to the transfer of the country. Nolin replied defiantly, which so angered Riel that he made a number of unaccountable arrests during the few following days, and even started out after Nolin, whose relatives, however, were so numerous,

Some Counter-Efforts and Their Results. 71

powerful and determined that Riel desisted in time to save himself from annihilation.

In the convention every phase of the country's future was discussed, and every question from railroad construction to a standing army was canvassed. A very elaborate Bill of Rights was framed and submitted to Commissioner Smith, who replied on behalf of the Dominion Government as far as he was able within the scope of his commission, after which he invited the convention to send delegates to confer with the authorities at Ottawa This invitation was accepted, and thus an important stage of progress was reached. One cannot study closely this portion of our country's history without feeling what a lasting debt the country owes to the courage, tact and patience of Mr. Donald A. Smith, who has been so deservedly raised to the peerage for his eminent services to the Empire.

It was not within the province of the convention, nor was it contemplated in the summons calling it, to take any steps towards confirming or approving the Provisional Government that Riel had already formed, but the opportunity was too good a one to be lost, and so he introduced the question when the other business was concluded. Most of the English delegates at once took the position that they had no instructions from their constituents on that point, and that therefore they could take no action upon it that would bind those who sent them to the convention; but Riel was anxious to have the matter pressed so that he would seem to have the approval of the country. The representatives from Kildonan, John Fraser and John Sutherland, declined to be parties to it till it seemed in the interests of present peace. They, having no time to consult their constituents, went to see Governor McTavish, and he, wearied with the protracted strife, said: " Form a government of some kind and restore peace and order in the settlement." And so with that end in view the delegates, without professing to bind their constituents, consented to the formation of a Provisional Government, whose *personnel* as to the chief officers was as stated above, though there was some hot feeling in the convention over continuing Riel in the presidency.

RIEL AND HIS COUNCIL (1869-70).

Le Roc. Pierre De Lorme. Thomas Bunn. Xavier Pagé. Andre Beauchemin. Baptiste Tereaux. John Bruce. Louis Riel. Bob O'Lone. W. B. O'Donoghue. Paul Proe. Francois Dauphinais. Thomas Spence. Pierre Poitras.

CHAPTER VI.

COLLAPSE OF THE REBELLION.

WHEN the Convention of the Forty adjourned they left such organization as undertook to carry on the government of the country, and from that time President Riel and his Council became the body that alleged to have the right to make and administer law in the community. Concurrently with the adjournment of the convention nearly all the remaining prisoners were released. The question as to why the English-speaking members of the convention did not refuse to sit except on the condition that they would all be released occurs most naturally here, and the only possible reply that can be given is that they had agreed to meet with the French and discuss the political situation, and that if they had withdrawn the latter would have remained and given the business whatever turn seemed pleasing to themselves, regardless of the views and wishes of any other portion of the community. But on the close of the convention the majority of the prisoners were released, and in all probability there would have been a general gaol delivery had not some developments taken place outside. Another warlike expedition began up the Assiniboine River, in Portage la Prairie, High Bluff, Poplar Point, White Horse Plains and Headingly, and a body of men numbering seventy-five or eighty, poorly enough armed, started on the march, intending to rendezvous at Kildonan and enlist the settlers along the Red River in the movement. The occasion of this was probably the delay in releasing the balance of the prisoners, and, on the part of the leaders, a certain amount of impatience with existing conditions. On the way down several of the houses were searched for Riel, who sometimes visited them, and though certain of those engaged in the search claimed that they only intended to hold him as a hostage for the release of the remaining prisoners, others openly said they would have made an end of him.

When this was reported to Riel he was once more at white heat. Many of his men had gone to their homes, but runners were quickly sent out, and until the counter-movements ceased Fort Garry was garrisoned by between six and seven hundred well-armed men—a force so great as to render attack by their poorly armed opponents on the stone-walled, bastioned and artilleried redoubt utterly futile. Nevertheless the body of men above referred to came on to Kildonan, where the most of them bivouacked in the historic church and school. I remember well when they arrived at the school, the morning of, I think, the 14th of February. The younger fry amongst us thought the whole thing a splendid idea, on the same principle that actuated the boy who fiercely rejoiced at the burning of his school because he did not know the geography lesson.

To the older people, doubtless, the situation was much more serious, and large numbers of men, not only from Kildonan, but also from St. Paul's, St Andrew's and St. Peter's, gathered together to discuss it. The consensus of opinion amongst them seems to have been that any movement of the kind contemplated would not only be futile, for the reasons above given, and likely to end in a useless shedding of blood, but that it was also inopportune, inasmuch as the species of union effected between the opposing parties by the convention just held would be the most certain means of preserving peace until the Dominion Government, with whom the delegates from that convention were treating, would take the whole matter in hand. In the meantime, those assembled at the rendezvous received every hospitality from the people of Kildonan, who entertained as many as they could in their homes, and provided food for those quartered in the church and school.

On the second day after the arrival of the party a very distressing incident took place in the shooting of one of the most promising young men in the parish. I remember as it were yesterday how one of the neighbor boys rushed into our house, exclaiming, "John Hugh Sutherland is shot!" and how the news fell upon us like lead. It appeared that on the night before a young French half-breed named Parisien, suspected of being one of Riel's spies, was taken prisoner by the men in the school-house, and the next day, when out with a guard he made a dash for liberty, snatching a double-barrelled gun from one of the sleighs as he went. He ran swiftly down the river-bank, and there met young Sutherland, who was riding on horseback toward the school. Parisien either feared that he would be intercepted, or perhaps he hoped to get the horse and so escape; but at any rate, he shot at Sutherland full in the breast. The horse swerved and the rider fell, but Parisien continued on. Looking back, he saw Sutherland rising to his feet, when, without stopping, he swung the gun over his shoulder (such was the deadly skill of these men) and discharged the second barrel, the contents entering the back of the unfortunate youth, who staggered and fell upon his face. Strong hands raised him and bore him to the hospitable manse of the Rev. John Black, near at hand, and on Sutherland's recovering consciousness and seeing the venerable face of his old minister, his first words were, " Pray for me." He lingered on into the night, and then one of the brightest lives of his time went out into the unseen with the prayer upon his lips, not for vengeance upon his murderer, but for mercy upon all. Meanwhile the horse, with empty and blood-stained saddle, had run back home to carry the tale to the parents; while the desperate spy, narrowly escaping lynching, lingered on to die from natural causes a few months afterwards. The effect of this lamentable affair was sobering in the extreme, and revealed, as by a startling providence, what might be the fate of others and what untold sorrow might come upon many homes without adequate cause and without commensurate results.

Some messages passed between Riel and the assembled force, and it seemed to be understood that the latter had liberty to return to their homes without any let or hindrance, and that the prisoners still held would be released. Accordingly, those gathered at Kildonan dispersed quietly to different parts of the parishes northward, but those from up the Assiniboine, who had begun the movement, did not fare so well. I have heard it said that Riel was angered at their exhibiting distrust of his word by making a detour to avoid passing Fort Garry, instead of going home by the usual travelled highway, but I think the story extremely improbable. It is more likely that he was enraged because some of those in the party were for the second time engaged in effort against him, and because, as referred to above, he had a lively idea of what might have befallen him had he been found by them on the way to the rendezvous. Whatever the reason may have been, the upshot was that as this handful of men were making their way to their homes across the deep snow of the prairie, they were intercepted by a large force of Riel's men, mounted and well armed. No resistance was made, as it was represented to them that Riel wished to see them at the fort, and they never dreamed of imprisonment. In any case, neither in numbers nor equipment would they have been any match for the rebels; but from personal acquaintance with many of those men, I feel sure that if they had known the indignities they were all to suffer, and if they could have seen the causeless and cruel murder of one of their number, they would have made then and there a last desperate stand against the enemy. As it was they went quietly to the fort, where to their surprise they were "thrust into the inner prison," and several of them—Boulton, Scott, Powers, McLeod, Alexander and George Parker—were specially singled out and the sentence of death by shooting suspended over their heads.

Riel was exceedingly desirous of securing the recognition of the Provisional Government by the English-speaking settlers, and took this method of forcing their hand, promising to spare the lives of these men if all the settlement would fall into line and send representatives to his "parliament." This, for the sake of peace, Special Commissioner Smith, aided by the clergy of various denominations, persuaded the people to do, and but for this it is exceedingly probable that Riel would have begun a series of murders whose end no one could foretell. Concerning Boulton (who was to do signal service in the field against his captor fifteen years later), Riel remained obdurate, and indeed decided that he should be shot on the night of the 19th of February, as having been the chief military director of the counter-movement. It has not been generally known, but the fact is that Boulton's life was finally spared at the intercession of Mr. (now Senator) and Mrs. Sutherland, of Kildonan, who had known Riel from his childhood, and who had come almost direct from the grave of their slain son to plead for the life of the condemned man. Riel was by no means without heart, and when he saw the earnestness as well as the grief of the parents, who had been so recently bereaved but who in their sorrow were thinking of others, he said, placing his hand upon the shoulder of the mother, "It is enough—he ought to die, but I will give you his life for the life of the son you have lost through these troubles."

And still the clouds had not all lifted. Riel's "parliament" met on the 26th of February, and to this, in the interests of peace, the English-speaking settlers, true to the promises they had made Commissioner Smith, sent representatives, who began forthwith to enact such legislation as the requirements of the time demanded. But there was withal a sullen feeling of unrest in the country, and a growing, even though unexpressed, discontent with the continued dominance and arbitrary methods of the so-called President, who played fast and loose with pledges and had such utterly un-British views as to the liberty of the subject. Doubtless Riel felt this atmosphere and tried a desperate remedy to change it, when on the 4th of March he caused the wanton murder of Thomas Scott, one of the prisoners.

I recall the first announcement of this tragedy made at a meeting in the Kildonan school by one who had come from Fort Garry that day —" There's been a man shot at the fort." That was all, until questioning drew from him such information as he had been able to gather; and that Riel had taken a mistaken means of impressing the settlers with his absolute authority was evidenced by the imprecations invoked upon his arrogant insolence. It is true that no means of taking steps to put an end to his lease of power were at hand, and as the best means in their judgment of keeping a madman quiet, the representatives of the settlers continued to sit in Council with the Provisional Government; but from that time the sympathy of the English-speaking people was completely estranged, and many of Riel's own class openly repudiated complicity with him in the killing of Scott.

Riel's paper, the *New Nation*, styled the murder of the young man a "military execution," and "regretted its necessity," which was said to be on account of Scott's alleged quarrelsome spirit which led him to insult the guard and even defy the President himself. There is no need now to canonize Scott, nor to claim that he possessed all the virtues and none of the vices of life; but so far as we can gather from those who knew him well, he was a young man of rather quiet habits, indisposed, as most men of Irish blood are, to be trodden upon, but not given to aggressive and unprovoked offending. Perhaps it was more by what we call chance than otherwise that he instead of Parker, or some of the others, was singled out for slaughter by the man who hoped through his death to strike terror into the community. It seems almost incredible now that after a mock trial, without any specified charges against the prisoner, without any opportunity for defence either in person or by counsel, against the protest and pleadings of the Rev. George Young, Commissioner Smith and others, a British subject in a British country should have been condemned to death and shot in the most brutal and bungling way at a few hours' notice.

However peacefully inclined one may be, he cannot picture the scene of the shooting and see this young man led out blindfolded to the shambles without feeling his blood move in fiercer thrills, and without adapting to the situation the sentiment of a verse written long ago in another connection:

> "Had I been there with sword in hand
>   And fifty Camerons by,
> That day through high Dunedin's streets
>   Had pealed the slogan cry.
>
> "Not all their troops of trampling horse
>   Nor might of mailèd men,
> Not all the rebels in the South
>   Had borne us backward then.
>
> "Once more his foot on Highland heath
>   Had trod as free as air,
> Or I, and all that I led on,
>   Been laid around him there."

Certain it is, as we have said, that from that hour the majority of people, however much they felt themselves obliged to remain passive, utterly disapproved of Riel's course; and some there were who told him to his face that for that and other reasons they would have nothing to do with him. Of this latter number was my father, as I recall from an incident that took place on the Queen's birthday, 1870. On the 20th of May, as appears from the files of the *New Nation*, he, with one or two others, was appointed by the Provisional Government a magistrate for the Fort Garry District. On May 24th the Queen's birthday was celebrated near Fort Garry with the usual sports, though it had been extensively reported that Riel was to seize the horses brought there for the races that he might have the best mounts for his cavalry. In the afternoon of that day I remember standing with my father on the roadside (now Main Street, Winnipeg) opposite the post-office, then kept by Mr. Bannatyne. It was quite customary in those days of limited correspondence and primitive postal facilities for the postmaster or his assistant to go out with a letter after anyone to whom it was addressed, as otherwise it might remain there uncalled for during many days. On this occasion Mr. Dan. Devlin, the assistant, seeing my father across the road, came over and handed him a large official envelope which had been recently dropped in the office. My father opened it, read the contents, and said to me, "We will go up to the fort." The envelope contained his commission from the Provisional Government as magistrate. He said little to me about it, as I was of but few years at the time; but I remember that, as we drove in through the gateway of Fort Garry, the guards were very polite to him, and one was detailed to hold his horse. My father went straight to the council-room, where Riel was found, and laid the commission down before the President.

"What is wrong with that?" asked Riel. "Isn't it properly signed and sealed? It is intended for you."

"I suppose it is properly signed," said my father, "but I do not wish to keep it. The fact is, Mr. Riel, I do not recognize your government as having any right or authority to make appointments like this. I am already a justice of the peace by the Queen's appointment through the Hudson's Bay Company, and so do not desire to keep this document, which has to me no value."

Riel seemed rather nettled, but brushed the paper aside with a "Very well, please yourself!" and then began to talk on other matters. Amongst other things, he said: "We had a Council meeting last night, and were talking about the soldiers who are coming from Canada. Poor fellows! they will have a hard time of it.

They will not reach here till the winter, and we were thinking of sending a party of men out to meet them with snowshoes." At this stage my father remarked that this would be needless trouble, as he thought they would be here sooner than some people wished. This did

LORD WOLSELEY.

not seem to improve matters much, and so shortly afterwards a somewhat ceremonious good-bye was said, and we drove away, the guards with much civility turning the horse and leading him out through the gates.

The summer wore on without much excitement, the prisoners having been all released, and the settlers going on with their usual work, while all the time looking eagerly for the troops. The first detachment of these, under Col. Wolseley (now Commander-in-Chief of the British army), arrived in the district on the 24th of August, when they came up the river and camped near Kildonan on their way to the fort. Many of the settlers went down to see them, but once they got within the picket lines they stayed there, much to their surprise, all night. Col. Wolseley, so far as he knew, was in the enemy's country, and was not going to run any risks from possible spies; hence every man that came within reach was held and examined by him. Of course, the people who were satisfied as to their own loyalty and knew nothing of military rules were considerably incensed, and one of the older men of the Selkirk settlers is said to have waxed perilously near the profane as he wrathfully assured the gallant Colonel that he was just as loyal as that commander himself. Wolseley, however, remained provokingly unmoved, and so quite a number of the settlers remained in "corral" till next morning, when he moved on to Fort Garry. I remember the day as one of drenching rain, when partly by boats on the river and partly by land as mounted scouts, the soldiers proceeded to the rebel stronghold. A goodly number of the settlers followed in their wake, expecting to see a "clash at arms," but they were all doomed to disappointment on that score, for when Wolseley's men reached the fort they found that Riel, O'Donoghue, Lepine and the rest had vacated in favor of the new-comers the very comfortable quarters they had occupied for so many months.

Hon. A. G. Archibald.   Hon. Alex. Morris.
Sir John Schultz.   Hon. David Laird.

EARLY GOVERNORS OF THE WEST.

CHAPTER VII.

THE MAKING OF A PROVINCE.

WITH the leading historical facts concerning the formative period immediately succeeding the first rebellion most of our readers will be more or less familiar, but they are only the centre of a great deal in the life that was unique and peculiar. On taking possession of Fort Garry Col. Wolseley very wisely refrained from assuming a military dictatorship, but called upon Mr. Donald A. Smith to act as the administrator of Government until the arrival and installation of the Hon. Adams G. Archibald, the first actual governor of the country under Canadian rule. The interregnum was not altogether devoid of excitement, nor were indeed many of the succeeding days commonplace or monotonously quiet.

For the maintenance of law and order a mounted police force was organized under command of Capt. Villiers, of the Quebec Rifles, and as this was the first regular police force in the West, and as some of the members in after years became prominent and wealthy men, we give the list in full: W. F. Alloway, James Cross, William Montgomery, Timothy Carroll, Edwin Doidge, Elijah Ketts, George Kerr, John Melanson, John Stevenson, Leon Hivet, George Nicol, H. Montgomery, Robert Power, Maxime Villebrun, W. Miller, John Paterson, Andrew Persy, Neil McCarthy, Michael Fox. These policemen had no sinecure, as may easily be imagined when the condition of things is considered.

The soldiers, released from the struggle of the half-military, half-voyageur life they had led for the past few months, were more or less disposed to take advantage of any opportunities that offered themselves for the somewhat fast and furious pace allowed by the codeless life of a frontier, and as they looked with some bitterness upon the half-breed population, as on those whose compatriots had imprisoned many and murdered one of their countrymen, conflicts more or less sharp were not infrequent on the streets of the straggling village. In one case a French half-breed, who had hot words with some of them in a saloon, was chased by an excited crowd to the river, and was there drowned in efforts to escape from them, though it was not likely they would have done him any serious injury. On another occasion a huge drummer had a pitched battle on the street with a French half-breed of colossal size and strength, who, however, having never been trained in the "manly art," succumbed to the superior skill of the new-comer.

One of the results of this latter encounter was that the aforesaid drummer established a notoriety as a fighter, thereby coming into demand for the stormy political meetings of that primitive time, and more than once have I seen him alert and ready to ply his pugilism at the signal of his political leader. Meetings of the kind indicated were not infrequent, as nearly every aspirant for political leadership was accompanied on his stumping tours by a "bully" with such help as he could gather, and I remember once seeing a meeting pass off peaceably, owing to the presence of the big drummer on the one side and an equally redoubtable champion on the other, each fearing to provoke active hostilities.

The beginnings of political life were crude enough. Governor Archibald simply chose a small "Cabinet" somewhat representative of the English and French elements in the community, then a census of the new province was rapidly taken, a distribution into constituencies was made, and the first election to the Local Legislature held. The Province was named Manitoba after the lake bearing that name, the word being derived from two Indian words, meaning together "the straits or narrows of the Great Spirit," and though usage has placed the accent on the third syllable, it should properly be pronounced with the accent on the last.

As "first things" are always of interest in later days, it might be well to say that the census in 1870 showed a population of 11,963 in the new province—of whom 1,565 were whites, 578 Indians, 5,757 French half-breeds, and 4,083 English half-breeds. There were 6,247 Catholics, 5,716 Protestants, and the nationalities of the whites were as follows: 747 born in the North-West, 294 in eastern Canada, 69 in the United States, 125 in England, 240 in Scotland, 47 in Ireland, 15 in France, and 28 in other countries. The first local election was held on the 30th December, 1870, and the following is a list of the members elected to the first Legislative Assembly of the Province of Manitoba, with the constituencies they represented:

Baie St. Paul............ Joseph Dubuc.
Headingly.............. John Taylor.

High Bluff	John Norquay.
Kildonan	John Sutherland.
Lake Manitoba	Angus McKay.
Poplar Point	David Spence.
Portage la Prairie	F. Bird.
St. Agathe	George Klyne.
St. Andrew's North ...	Alfred Boyd.
St. Andrew's South ...	E. H. G. G. Hay.
St. Anne	J. H. McTavish.
St. Boniface East	M. A. Girard.
St. Boniface West	Louis Schmidt.
St. Charles	Henry J. Clarke.
St. Clement's	Thomas Bunn.
St. Francois Xavier East	Pascal Breland.
St. Francois Xavier West	Joseph Royal.
St. James'	E. Burke.
St. Norbert North	Joseph Lemay.
St. Norbert South	Pierre Delorme.
St. Paul's	Dr. C. J. Bird.
St. Peter's	Thomas Howard.
St. Vital	A. Beauchemin.
Winnipeg	Donald A. Smith.

The first regularly constituted Government consisted of the following members:

Hon. Henry J. Clarke, Q.C., Attorney-General.

Hon. Marc Amable Girard, Treasurer.

Hon. Thomas Howard, Secretary.

Hon. Alfred Boyd, Public Works and Agriculture.

Hon. James McKay, without portfolio.

It was some years before party politics could be developed, and hence, during the meetings above referred to, the questions discussed were of a very local character, and in the end the candidate who had the largest family connection in the neighborhood was generally elected. For some time rebellion echoes were heard at all the meetings, like the war issues in United States politics, and in the English-speaking constituencies any suspected complicity in the misdeeds of the past and any heresy as to the amnesty of the rebel leaders would contribute powerfully to the overthrow of the suspected party. These meetings were not without their humorous side, and ofttimes somewhat peculiar situations arose out of the unfamiliarity of the settlers with the methods and expressions of parliamentary debate. I recollect once when a school-teacher had framed a motion and made a speech as to the leniency with which we should view those who, as mere *dupes*, had been drawn into the rebellion, that the reporter gave out that he had made a motion as to the *brutes* who had gone into the rebellion. The chagrin of the school-teacher may be imagined. I also recall seeing a man who had occupied the chair during a meeting leaving it in high dudgeon on a motion to vacate, which he was not aware was made preparatory to moving him a vote of thanks. On another occasion one embryo statesman, who was holding before his audience the hope of some change in governmental methods, and who sought to clinch his speech by the use of a proverb, got the two sayings, "Every dog has his day" and "It's a long lane that has no turning" slightly mixed, and vehemently assured the people that "It was a long dog that had no turning."

The voting was all done openly, and hence it was not surprising that in the older settled districts an election threw apples of discord into regions where formerly the inhabitants had lived in peace and quietness, while the ties which frequently occurred during the polling-day sent the pulse of the community up to fever pitch. Canvassing was of the most personal kind, and as we then had no legislation in regard to corrupt practices to reveal the sin, it was considered a sign of meanness on the part of a candidate not to provide a somewhat elaborate meal at every committee meeting, and ample refreshments in some house near the polling-place on election day. Riots were not altogether unknown and at the first election in Winnipeg wagon-spokes were freely used, the Chief of Police was rendered *hors de combat*, a printing office was wrecked, and finally the military had to be called out to overawe the noisy multitude.

When the first legislature met, it could not reasonably be expected that the same dignity and decorum, the same acquaintance with parliamentary methods or the same breadth of statesmanship would be manifested as in older lands. The appearance of the early House was peculiar and characteristic of a transition stage. I recall seeing in the old legislative chamber men clothed in the faultless Prince Albert black beside men in a curious compound of the old and the new, having the long curled hair of raven hue, wearing the moccasins to which they had always been accustomed and which certainly had the advantage of silence over creaky boots; coats open, displaying the colored flannel shirt without a collar, and across the waist, picturesquely slashed, the French belt or sash commonly worn on the prairies. The literary education of some of these men had been of the scantiest, and when one day a member sent a note across the floor asking a member of the Government to move the House into a " committy of the hole," it was taken jocularly as a deep-laid plot to entrap the Executive unawares. In a case under my own observation a newly-elected member, whose sudden elevation had induced the too free use of stimulants, was making himself so obnoxious that he had to be sharply called to order by the Speaker with threats of expulsion from the precincts. The member, unabashed, told the Speaker, in effect, that he ought to remember the primitive condition of things in the country; and desiring to impress the Speaker with the fact that though he (the member) was not a finished statesman, he was fairly representative of, if not superior to, his constituents in attainments, said : " You may think I am a fool, Mr. Speaker, but I am not such a fool as the people who sent me here ;" in which saying the member builded better than he knew, and aptly described what has been witnessed frequently enough in political life.

That early House, too, had, in the person of a member of great avoirdupois, an inveterate joker, who, being something of an artist, used to sketch his fellow-members in their various attitudes and confront them with the pictures that they might see themselves as others saw them. Notwithstanding these peculiarities much solid work was done and many a thrilling speech made. The foundations were laid in much good legislation, and special attention was given to the religious, educational and benevolent projects of the time. Back there the enactments that gave rise to the famous School Question were passed, though it is no secret now that the House had no intention of committing the young province to the dual system of schools abolished by the famous statutes of 1890. Proceedings were conducted in the Legislature, the courts, etc., in both English and French for many years, and one of the most impassioned and eloquent speeches of the time was made by a Frenchman on behalf of retaining his mother tongue in public and official use; albeit that same speech was made in English, and the absurdity of wasting time and money in using two languages in a British country, where all who took an intelligent interest in affairs spoke English, soon became apparent. Moreover, it was found that while the appropriation was duly made, there were cases in which the French printing of the proceedings was not done for years after the sessions of the House. There was, too, a somewhat ridiculous side to the matter. Speeches from the throne were always read in both languages. Some of the governors could read in both; others, who only read English, had the good sense to hand the speech for reading to the French clerk; but when English-speaking governors, for fear of shattering the Constitution, persisted in reading the French speech with English pronunciation, the effect was so distressing that the French themselves were doubtless glad when their beautiful language could no longer be mangled so heartlessly before the public.

Changes other than the abolition of the dual language system were also made at an early date. "Dualities" have had a hard time in the West, for shortly after the beginning of our history dual representation in local and Dominion Houses had to succumb. Next in order the "Upper House" was forced to go.

The Legislative Council (as our "Upper House" was called) had come into existence on the 10th March, 1871, and was composed of the following gentlemen appointed by the Lieutenant-Governor in Council: Hons. Donald Gunn, Francois Dauphinais, Solomon Hamelin, Colin Inkster, Dr. J. H. O'Donnell, Francis Ogletree and James McKay, the latter being Speaker of the House. This institution, intended, I suppose, as "a check on hasty legislation," was not easily annihilated, for the members in full enjoyment of its titles and emoluments were not likely to approve any bill for their own decapitation: but after some new appointments the body finally lapsed out of existence by the casting vote of the Speaker. It was only by degrees that the party element came into western politics. The natives of the country had no hereditary tendencies in that direction, but gradually the presence of Federal differences began to be felt in local circles, and under

HON. DONALD GUNN.

that pressure men were soon found arrayed in opposing lines of battle. Amongst the politicians of the early years were many who had won their spurs in the older provinces, and whose names will be in memory there; but of those indigenous to the soil of Manitoba were several who took a prominent part in shaping the destinies of their native land, and around these more especially interest for our present purpose centres.

In this number by far the most prominent and powerful figure was that of John Norquay, a man who made his influence felt far beyond provincial bounds. He was what was called a Scotch half-breed, uniting in himself the strain of the Orkneys with a mixture of Indian blood which he was always proud to own. He was educated wholly at the Anglican school and college at St. John's, through the benevolence of the Church, became a school-teacher in early life, and at the first local election became a member of the Local Legislature, and so remained till his death in 1891. For some seventeen years he was a member of the Government, and during nearly all that time he was First Minister of his native province. Physically, he was a man of tremendous size and strength, standing some six feet three in height, and broad and strong in proportion. As an indication of his physique, I recall seeing him at a political meeting, when a fight was imminent, thrust himself between the combatants, who found themselves as much apart as if a rock had dropped between them. He must have been a diligent student to secure the complete mastery of English he manifested in his public addresses, as well as the thorough acquaintance with public questions that gave his speeches authority. As a speaker he was at his best. He had a voice of clear and resonant force, and a fluency which carried everything before it without degenerating into wordiness, while his vocabulary was that of one who had gained it by wide reading and keen study. I heard him speak on almost every kind of theme, on a great variety of platforms, and never knew him to disappoint the expectations of his listeners. Wherever he spoke in the native parishes he would naturally have a specially sympathetic audience; but as an example of his influence on other audiences, I remember hearing him speak with great effect in an immense hall in St. Paul, Minnesota, on the occasion of a concert given there during an ice carnival by the St. George's Snowshoe Club, of Winnipeg. He was on his way home from Ottawa to Winnipeg when we secured him at St. Paul, knowing that his presence would redeem our concert from possible failure. The gathering of several thousands was representative of many parts of the United States, that nation of public speakers, and they looked with somewhat critical gaze upon our burly Premier

HON. JOHN NORQUAY.

when he was introduced as an extra on the programme. He had no special text given him, but dwelt chiefly upon the friendly relations and close connection which had always subsisted between the Red River colonists and the cities of the western States, whence he passed to the wider questions of international fellowship, evoking rounds of applause by the rolling periods of his eloquence.

In his home life, John Norquay was a lovable man, and I have more than once seen him lay aside the cares of state and play like a school-boy with his children, who clambered delightedly upon his stalwart person. His tenure of political power closed in 1889, when, weakened from without by conflicts with the Federal authorities on questions of provincial rights as to railway advantages and other matters, and from within by the overcrowding of government departments by men to whom he was too good-natured to say "no," he resigned the premiership into the charge of Dr. Harrison, who shortly afterwards met defeat at the hands of the Greenway-Martin forces. At the next session, Mr. Norquay returned to the House as leader of a "corporal's guard" in Opposition. His speech in self-defence, as he stood almost alone like a wounded stag at bay, remains as the one passage of genuine and lofty eloquence that has echoed in the halls of our Legislature. In that speech he reviewed his long tenure of office, without claiming infallibility, but showing how, with abundant opportunity for enriching himself, he had surrendered in comparative poverty the seals of office, and declaring how he was satisfied in being able to hand down an unsullied name to his children. During the delivery of his speech a member thoughtlessly taunted him with his Indian blood, and few will forget the thrillingly dramatic effect of Mr. Norquay's action as he threw up his hand to reveal the dark skin of which he said he was proud, and how he sent back with stunning force a rebuke for the unhappy sneer.

Not many months after that Mr. Norquay died of a sudden inflammation. The recollection is yet vivid of how the news sped to the startled hearts of the people, and of the way in which, regardless of party, they united in mourning for one who had done signal service to the Province in which he was born. The Greenway Government gave him a state funeral, and friends all over Canada contributed to the erection of the handsome monument which stands over his dust in the old graveyard at St. John's. No claim is made by anyone that he was a faultless man, nor even that he could have taken the highest place in the highest sphere, but considering his opportunities and the lateness of the hour in his life when he came, without any experience whatsoever, into the new career of politics, John Norquay's name stands as that of one of the most remarkable men we have yet seen in Canada.

Beside Mr. Norquay for some years in public life stood another of the native-born, the Hon. A. M. Sutherland, a brother of the young man who was shot by one of Riel's spies during the first rebellion, as already recorded. One of my first recollections of Sutherland goes back to a day at the Kildonan school in 1870, when a boy came over to the icy play-ground and said, "Aleck Sutherland has come to attend school." When the bell rang and the school assembled we saw, with the admiring gaze of small boys, a powerfully built, broad-shouldered, athletic and handsome man, who had come back to school after years of absence with the view of receiving higher education and going on to the legal profession. And so in that school, in Manitoba College and in Toronto University he pursued his studies to graduation, and in due time was admitted to the practice of law in Winnipeg. During his law studies he ran for the Local Legislature in Kildonan, his birthplace, was elected and re-elected, holding the seat till his death in 1884, and in the meantime occupying the posts of Attorney-General and Provincial Secretary with marked success. His most outstanding characteristic was a manly straightforwardness which made him a universal favorite, a fair, if forcible opponent, and a factor in a political contest that no one could ignore. His untimely death cut short what would doubtless have been a notable career, and the letters from all quarters that poured in upon his sorrowing parents, to the size of a small volume, were an index of the esteem in which he was held far and wide.

At the time of the death of Mr. Sutherland, John MacBeth, an almost inseparable personal friend, held the position of Clerk of the Executive Council, which he unselfishly resigned at the call of his leader, Mr. Norquay, to contest the constituency of Kildonan, he being also a native of that parish. He was elected for the unexpired term, and returned again at the following election, holding the seat till a redistribution took place, when he, with equal loyalty and unselfishness, retired in favor of Mr.

Norquay, who contested the new division. His warmth of heart completely disarmed the personal enmity of his bitterest political opponents, so that when the news of his death, which took place in October, 1897, reached Manitoba, there were found amongst his most sincere mourners many to whom he had stood diametrically opposed on many a hotly contested political battlefield.

In the history of every country there are found the names of some who have apparently taken but a small part in public affairs, and are soon forgotten in the rush of events, but who, nevertheless, formed an important link in the chain of the country's progress; and as I look back over the death-roll of Manitoba, the somewhat obscure name of F. H. Francis appears as one occupying this unique place. Mr. Francis was an Englishman by birth, an educated and cultured man, and a fluent speaker as far as delicate health permitted. When Mr. Norquay resigned the premiership in favor of his colleague, Dr. Harrison, the latter took into his Cabinet as representative of the French element, Mr. Burk, a merchant at St. Charles, who offered himself for re-election in the constituency of St. Francois Xavier. To oppose him with all the Government prestige and patronage at his back seemed a forlorn hope, but the then Opposition persuaded Mr. Francis to make the effort. It was in Mr. Francis' favor that he was equally at home in speaking English or French, and that as a merchant within the constituency he personally knew nearly all the electors. It is

HON. F. H. FRANCIS.

almost certain that he was the only man at that time who could gain sufficient support from the different elements to defeat Mr. Burk, as he did, to the great surprise of the Government.

By that defeat the Harrison Government was overturned, the present Greenway administration took office, and ere long the famous school question, which changed the political face of all Canada, came into being. I have had many conversations with people who took part in that election, but there seems to be a great divergence of opinion as to what actually took place in regard to this special matter. It appears certain that for some reason or other the Harrison party assured the electors that if the Greenway party succeeded the French Roman Catholic Separate Schools would be abolished, and as to what the Greenway party said in reply there is remarkable lack of unanimity. What really took place during the election is matter of controversy, but not many days elapsed thereafter before Mr. Joseph Martin, the Attorney-General in the new administration, announced the intention of the Government to abolish Separate Schools and inaugurate a national system, which was accordingly done by the now famous Act of 1890. The St. Francois Xavier election, which was won by Mr. Francis, was the pivotal point in the whole matter.

Another of Mr. Francis's achievements was the building of the Deaf and Dumb Institute, now one of the best equipped institutions in the Province. At an early stage in the session he secured a commission to take a census of the deaf and dumb in the Province, and thereafter, even at his own expense, secured rooms and a teacher, but lived to see this work for the unfortunate on which he had set his heart an accomplished and successful fact. And so with only a few months of political life, for

HON. JOSEPH MARTIN, Q.C.

which he had no special love, Mr. Francis was able to bring about changes with results of extraordinarily far-reaching character. Other names of those who took part in the formative period of our history readily occur, but of these I have little personal reminiscence, while any detailed sketches of our living statesmen on both sides of politics are omitted for obvious reasons.

Amongst the Dominion statesmen who have gone from us the name of the late Sir John Schultz survives with the foremost by reason of his commanding ability and his close connection with the most stirring events of our history. What we have already written in regard to him will give some idea of his striking appearance, his loyalty, his indomitable will and courage. But we would be giving an imperfect portrait of him did we not cause him to stand out in the memory of the country he loved as a man of culture and refinement as well as of courage and strength. As a public speaker he excelled by reason of his perfect coolness, his musical, well-modulated voice, his choice language and clear-headed statesmanship. As a member of the House of Commons he exerted great influence on all legislation affecting this country, and did much to direct the attention of Canada to the great domain now being opened up in the far North-West. The knighthood conferred upon him was a fitting recognition of the perils and sufferings he had undergone in the country's service, to the complete ruin of a once splendid constitution. While Lieutenant-Governor of Manitoba he did signal service in the way of inculcating lessons of patriotism amongst the school children of the Province, as well as by throwing the full weight of his influence on the side of temperance and other moral reforms. In private life he was courtly and graceful, considerate of the comfort and feelings of those he met, and from an abundant store of information always a ready and interesting conversationalist. From intimate intercourse with him in the closing years of his life I was given to feel that he was realizing to the full the earnestness of life with all its opportunities, and the solemnity of being called upon to exert an influence on one's day and generation.

Back somewhat farther in the history of the West we find the name of the late Hon. James McKay, of Silver Heights, as one who, in the interests of Canada, wielded a marked influence on the country when it was passing from the old to the new. He was what we call a Scotch half-breed, his father a Scotchman who had taken a share in one of the Sir John Franklin expeditions, and his mother having the blood of the French and the Cree in her veins. As I remember James McKay, in the last decade of his life, he was a man of immense size and weight, but his width of shoulder and general strength were so extraordinary that he seemed to carry himself lightly enough. From early custom on the plains he always wore moccasins, and I have seen somewhere a note by a traveller who met him in the corridor of a hotel, and who could not help contrasting the soft footfall of the magnificently massive man with the noisy step of some fussy little body who passed with creaking boots at the same time. McKay was a member of some of the early Cabinets, and afterwards Speaker of the Legislative Council in Manitoba, but his contribution to the national history was not made so much in legislative halls as out on his native prairies in connection with the treaties arranged between the Government and the Indians all over the West. He knew the Indians and they knew him, hence he became a medium of communication, ensuring the conclusion of treaties wise, humane and lasting. The Dominion will never wholly realize how much of the comparative peace she has enjoyed on the vast plains of the West she owes to the statesmanship of Governors Morris and Laird, aided by such men as James McKay, the Revs. John McKay, George McDougall, Father Lacombe, and others whom the Indians loved and trusted. The last time I recall seeing James McKay was during Lord Dufferin's visit to this country in 1877, when in Deer Park, near his own place, McKay was master of ceremonies in a reception to the Governor-General which took the form of a wild-west entertainment. McKay had a buffalo herd there, with broncho-breakers from the frontier, and as the massive man drove his famous cream horse here and there to regulate matters, the Governor-General perhaps realized the peculiar value of having such men to stand between the old life and the new—a fact to

REV. GEORGE M'DOUGALL.

which he made reference afterwards in many a public address. Through the action of a limited number of them, many people think of the name "half-breed" only in connection with western rebellions, whereas the real history shows that the presence of men with Indian blood in their veins has been a most important factor in the peaceful making of the West into a part of Canada.

CHAPTER VIII.

CONTACT WITH THE OUTSIDE WORLD.

FROM the earliest times the question of communication with the outside world had been a burning problem. The first settlers, who had begun their isolation by failing to hear of Waterloo for long months after that famous battle took place, had become more or less reconciled to living "far from the madding crowd's ignoble strife." These pioneers grew content with the bi-annual trip to York Factory for merchandise and mail, and with the commerce and communication that percolated through the western States. They were not quite so solitary as the Hudson's Bay Company's officer at a remote point, who received his copies of the London *Times* once a year with the annual packet, and who began always at the farthest back number and read right through to get abreast of events, though even then he left off about a year behind. But while the condition of the first settlers was, soon after their arrival, a little better than his, it was not wholly satisfactory to the growing colony on the Red River, and especially was it unsatisfactory to those who in the sixties began to come more rapidly into the settlement. Hence, as soon as the rebellion had quieted down, people began to look around for inlets for population and merchandise and outlets for produce. The old steamboat, flat-bottomed and stern-wheeled, was one of the prized institutions of the time. It ran from near the "head waters" in the western States down the Red River to Fort Garry, and on rare occasions down past the lower settlement to Lower Fort Garry. These latter occasions were red-letter days for the community: schools were dismissed while the boat was passing, and grown-up people gathered on the banks, greeting her with shotgun salutes, and eliciting responses from the boat whistle, to the half-terror, half-delight of the children. When merchants began to open stores in some numbers on the present site of Winnipeg, the advent of "the first boat" after the long winter was the goal to which the hopes and the longings of people most turned. The merchant of to-day who has "just sold out," but assures the customer that he has some of the desired goods "on the way," is distinctly of the same genus as the ancient and veracious merchants of Winnipeg, who invariably asserted concerning everything that they did not have on hand, that "it would be in on the first boat." Some mathematical genius, who perhaps desired to keep his mind engaged in arithmetical gymnastics during the long winter, made much inquiry for goods, keeping note of the stereotyped reply, and towards spring gave in miles what he considered the dimensions of "the first boat" would be if the promises of the merchants had any tangible foundation.

One of the first indications we had of swifter communication with the outside world was the erection of telegraph poles and lines across our farms in the early seventies. The proceedings were more or less shrouded with that mystery and occultness which provokes the inquiry of boys; and like the man who, seeing the electric light for the first time, wondered "how they could get such light from a hairpin in a bottle," we used to wonder how men sent messages on those wires twisted round a "bottle" at intervals. We tried to examine as far as possible, and although warned as to the danger of meddling with the strange machinery, some boy of sure eye and hand would knock one of the "bottles" off occasionally; but it refused to yield up the secret of telegraphy, and replacing it, we would take our seats upon the fence and watch whether any of the daring birds that took their places on the wires would be "shot" by the passing telegrams.

LORD DUFFERIN.

By degrees railroads pushed their way westward through the States to the boundary line, and the Pembina branch of the Canadian Pacific Railway was built to connect with Winnipeg in 1878. The first spikes in this road were driven in September, 1877, by the Governor-General and the Countess of Dufferin, whose visit in that year to the North-West marks a new era in the history of the country. They came by way of Toronto, Chicago and St. Paul, taking the last stage of the journey from Fisher's Landing to Fort Garry on the steamer *Minnesota*. They were received with unbounded enthusiasm in the new West, and there, as elsewhere, the tactful Governor-General did much to oil the machinery of Confederation and remove particles likely to cause friction. They had many unique experiences during their tour and their camping out, amongst them being shooting the Grand Rapids above Lake Winnipeg in a York boat, and riding in a Red River cart drawn by thirty garlanded oxen at Stony Mountain. The speech given by Lord Dufferin at a dinner in Winnipeg, before returning east, has always been regarded as one of the best immigration agencies the West has had, and we give a portion of it as bearing on the subject in hand. On rising Lord Dufferin said :

"*Mr. Mayor, Your Honor, Ladies and Gentlemen :*

"In rising to express my acknowledgments to the citizens of Winnipeg for thus crowning the friendly reception I have received throughout the length and breadth of Manitoba by so noble an entertainment, I am painfully impressed by the consideration of the many respects in which my thanks are due to you and to so many other persons in the Province. From our first landing on your quays until the present moment, my progress through the country has been one continual delight, nor has the slightest hitch or incongruous incident marred the satisfaction of my visit. I have to thank you for the hospitalities I have enjoyed at the hands of your individual citizens, as well as of individual communities—for the tasteful and ingenious decorations which adorned my route —for the quarter of a mile of evenly-yoked oxen that drew our triumphal car—for the universal proofs of your loyalty to the throne and to the Mother Country, and for your personal good-will to Her Majesty's representative. Above all, I have to thank you for the evidences produced on either hand along our march of your prosperous condition, of your perfect contentment, of your confidence in your future homes; for I need not tell you that to anyone in my situation, smiling cornfields, cosy homesteads, the joyful faces of prosperous men and women, and the laughter of healthy children are the best of all triumphal adornments.

"But there are other things for which I ought to be obliged to you; and first, for the beautiful weather you have taken the precaution to provide us with during some six weeks of perpetual camping out, for which attention I have received Lady Dufferin's especial orders to render you her personal thanks— an attention which the phenomenon of a casual waterspout enabled us only the better to appreciate;

and lastly, though certainly not least, for not having generated amongst you that fearful entity, 'a Pacific Railway question'—at all events not in those dire and tragic proportions in which I have encountered it elsewhere. Of course, I know a certain phase of the railway question is agitating even this community, but it has assumed the mild character of a domestic rather than an inter-provincial controversy. Two distinguished members, moreover, of my government have been lately amongst you, and have doubtless acquainted themselves with your views and wishes. It is not necessary, therefore, that I should mar the hilarious character of the present festival by any untimely allusions to so grave a matter.

"Well, then, ladies and gentlemen, what am I to say and do to you in return for all the pleasure and satisfaction I have received at your hands? I fear there is very little that I can say, and scarcely anything that I can do commensurate with my obligations. Stay! There is one thing, I think, I have already done for which I am entitled to claim your thanks. You are doubtless aware that a great political controversy has for some time raged between the two great parties of the State as to which of them is responsible for the visitation of that terror of two continents—the Colorado bug. The one side is disposed to assert that if their opponents had never acceded to power the Colorado bug would never have come to Canada. I have reason to believe, however, though I know not whether any substantial evidence has been adduced in support of this assertion, that my government deny and repudiate having any sort of concert or understanding with that irresponsible invader. It would be highly unconstitutional if I, who am bound to hold an impartial balance between the contending parties of the State, were to pronounce an opinion upon this momentous question. But, however disputable a point may be the prime and original authorship of the Colorado bug, there is one fact no one will question, namely, that to the presence of the Governor-General in Manitoba is to be attributed the sudden, total, otherwise unaccountable, and, I trust, permanent disappearance, not only from this province, but from the whole North-West, of the infamous and unmentionable 'hopper,' whose visitations in the past have proved so distressing to the agricultural interests of the entire region.

"But apart from being the fortunate instrument of conferring this benefit upon you, I fear the only further return in my power is to assure you of my great sympathy with you in your endeavors to do justice to the material advantages with which your Province has been so richly endowed by the hand of Providence. From its geographical position and its peculiar characteristics, Manitoba may be regarded as the keystone of that mighty arch of sister provinces which spans the continent from the Atlantic to the Pacific. It was here that Canada, emerging from her woods and forests, first gazed upon her rolling prairies and unexplored North-West, and learned, as by an unexpected revelation, that her historical territories of the Canadas, her eastern seaboards of New Brunswick, Labrador and Nova Scotia, her Laurentian lakes and valleys, lowlands and pastures, though themselves more extensive than half a dozen European kingdoms, were but the vestibules and ante-chambers to that till then undreamed-of Dominion, whose illimitable dimensions confound the arithmetic of the surveyors and the verification of the explorer. It was hence that, counting her past achievements as but the preface and prelude to her future exertions and expanding destinies, she took a new departure, received the afflatus of a more important inspiration, and felt herself no longer a mere settler along the banks of a single river, but the owner of half a continent, and in the magnitude of her possession, in the wealth of her resources, in the sinews of her material might, the peer of any power on earth. In a recent remarkably witty speech the Marquis of Salisbury alluded to the geographical misconceptions often engendered by the smallness of the maps upon which the figure of the world is depicted. To this cause is probably to be attributed the inadequate opinion of well-educated persons of the extent of Her Majesty's North American possessions. Perhaps the best way of correcting such a universal misapprehension would be by a summary of the rivers which flow through them, for we know that as a poor man cannot afford to live in a big house, so a small country cannot support a big river. Now, to an Englishman or a Frenchman, the Severn or the Thames, the Seine or the Rhone would appear considerable streams, but in the Ottawa, a mere affluent of the St. Lawrence—an affluent, moreover, which reaches the parent stream six hundred miles from its mouth—we have a river nearly five hundred and fifty miles long, and three or four times as big as any of them. But even after having ascended the St. Lawrence itself to Lake Ontario, and pursued it across lakes Erie, St. Clair, Huron and Superior to Thunder Bay, a distance of one thousand five hundred miles, where are we? In the estimation of the person who has made the journey, at the end of all things; but to us, who know better, scarcely at the commencement of the great fluvial system of the Dominion, for from that spot, that is to say, from Thunder Bay, we are at once able to ship our astonished traveller on to the Kaministiquia, a river some hundred miles long. Thence, almost in a straight line, we launch him upon Lake Shebandowan and Rainy Lake and River, a magnificent stream three hundred yards broad and a couple of hundred miles long, down whose tranquil bosom he floats into the Lake of the Woods, where he finds himself on a sheet of water which, though diminutive as compared with the inland seas he has left behind him, will probably be found sufficiently extensive to make him fearfully sea-sick during his passage across it. For the last eighty miles, however, he will be consoled by sailing through a succession of land-locked channels, the beauty of whose scenery, while it resembles, certainly excels the far-famed Thousand Islands of the St. Lawrence. From this lacustrine paradise of sylvan beauty we are able at once to transfer our friend to the Winnipeg, a river whose existence in the very heart and centre of the continent is in itself one of nature's most delightful miracles, so beautiful and varied are its rocky banks, its tufted islands; so broad, so deep, so fervid is the volume of its waters, the extent of their lake-like expansions, and the tremendous power of their rapids. At last, let us suppose we have landed our *protégé* at the town of Winnipeg, the half-way house of the continent, the capital of the Prairie Province, and, I trust, the future 'umbilicus' of the Dominion. Having now had so much of water, having now reached the home of the buffalo, like Falstaff he naturally 'babbles of green fields' and careers in imagination over the primeval grasses of the prairie. Not at all. Escorted by Mr. Mayor and the Town Council we take him down to your quay, and ask him which he will ascend first, the Red River or the Assiniboine—two streams, the one five hundred miles long, the other four hundred and eighty, which so happily mingle their waters within your city limits. After having given him a preliminary canter on these respective rivers, we take him off to Lake Winnipeg, an inland sea three hundred miles long and upwards of sixty broad, during the navigation of which for many a weary hour he will find himself out of sight of land, and probably a good deal more indisposed than ever he was on the Lake of the Woods or even the Atlantic. At the north-west angle of Lake Winnipeg he hits upon the mouth of the Saskatchewan, the gateway to the North-West, and the starting point to another one thousand five hundred miles of navigable water flowing nearly due east and west between its alluvial banks. Having now reached the Rocky Mountains, our 'ancient mariner,' for by this time he will be quite entitled to such an appellation, knowing that water cannot run up hill, feels certain his aquatic experiences are concluded. He was never more mistaken. We immediately launch him upon the Athabasca and Mackenzie rivers, and start him on a longer trip than he has yet ever taken, the navigation of the Mackenzie River alone exceeding two thousand five hundred miles. If he survives this last experience, we wind up his peregrinations by a concluding voyage down the Fraser River, or, if he prefers it, the Thompson River, to the coast; whence, having provided him with a first-class ticket for that purpose, he will probably prefer getting home by the Canadian Pacific.

"Now, in this enumeration, those who are acquainted with the country know that, for the sake of brevity, I have omitted thousands of miles of other lakes and rivers which water various regions of the North-West, the Qu'Appelle River, Belly River, Lake Manitoba, the Winnipegosis, Shoal Lake, etc, along which I might have dragged, and finally exterminated, our way-worn guest. But the sketch I have given is more than sufficient for my purpose; and when it is further remembered that the most of these streams flow for their entire length through alluvial plains of the richest description, where year after year wheat can be raised without manure, or any sensible diminution in its yield, and where the soil everywhere presents the appearance of a highly cultivated suburban kitchen-garden in England, enough has been said to display the agricultural richness of the territories I have referred to, and the capabilities they possess of affording happy and prosperous homes to millions of the human race."

After referring to the many different nationalities composing the population of the West, to the problems yet to arise, and dwelling eloquently upon the future destiny of the Dominion, Lord Dufferin closed a great speech by expressing the hope that the finances of the country would soon provide for the West a railway to carry out the surplus produce, " which," said he, " my own eyes have seen imprisoned in your storehouses for want of the means of transport." The Governor-General's hope in this regard soon found fruition.

This was the decade when efforts were made to construct a transcontinental line through

Canadian territory by utilizing "the magnificent water stretches," of which the Governor-General had spoken so eloquently, and hence eastward from Winnipeg beginnings were made somewhat to the bewilderment of the old settlers, through whose growing crops the roadway of the iron horse was relentlessly pushed. The Federal Government of the day felt inclined to cross the Red River about twenty-two miles north of Winnipeg, where the picturesque town of Selkirk now stands at the head of Lake Winnipeg navigation, but to that course it was objected that crossing at Selkirk would ignore the growing centre at Winnipeg, would miss the fertile plains just west of that city, as well as necessitate the great expense of construction over certain districts north-west of Selkirk, where morasses alleged to be bottomless existed. However that might be, the fact is that Winnipeg eventually drew the main line of the great railway through her borders. Not many of us have found common ground on all points with Mr. Debs, but most of us will agree with him in preferring Government ownership of railroads to railroad ownership of Governments; and yet in the light of the history of the time we know that it was not till the Canadian Pacific Railway had passed out of the immediate control of the Government

into the hands of a company that its construction
and operation became a success. That may be to
the discredit of the Government and to the credit
of the company, as the case may be, but I am
now simply stating the fact. It is true that the
company received from the country an enormous
bonus in money and lands, but it should not be
forgotten that they faced enormous difficulty in
attempting to build a road, offering the most
amazing engineering problems, across a vast
area of country at that time only partially
settled, and a great part of which will, so far
as we see, remain unsettled and non-producing
for all time. It was, perhaps, fortunate that
most of the Canadian directorate hailed from
the land of the saying, "a stout heart to a stey
brae," and few who know the way in which
these men pledged their private fortunes and
hazarded their business reputations will grudge
the joy that must have been theirs when one of
the most distinguished of their number, Sir
Donald A. Smith, at Craig Ellachie, in 1885,
drove the last spike in the band uniting oceans
which lave the opposite shores of Canada. In
fact, one cannot read the name of the place
amidst the great mountain ranges where that
notable act was done without thinking of the
legends of Highland seers concerning the "grey

frontlet of rock" which stood in the glen of Strathspey, and from whose summit the scattered firs and wind-swept heather in war time whispered to the clansmen, "Stand fast," for only by the most determined steadfastness could men have completed the task of which we have just spoken.

It was for some time quite fashionable to denounce the rapid construction of the C.P.R. as conducing to the scattering of population westward, and to say that the road should have been built by easy stages, and settlement consolidated in lateral directions. Apart from the fact that such a process would have been oblivious of the conditions upon which British Columbia entered Confederation, there was only a modicum of truth in the assertion that slower construction of the railway would have consolidated settlement, as early settlers who witnessed the movement of population can testify. There seems always to have been a westward moving instinct in humanity, and under its influence men have, from the beginning, been crowding towards the setting sun. In the West, long before a railway was dreamed of, I saw my own kith and kin leave the Red River colony to travel, amidst great difficulty, with cart-trains, five hundred miles north-westward and form a settlement there. Those who were in the country at the time know that during the construction of the C. P. R. emigrants left its trains at the various termini, and, loading their effects on "prairie schooners," pushed on, leaving good land unoccupied to the right hand and to the left.

For several years the Canadian Pacific Railway was the only railroad traversing the prairies west of Winnipeg. Then the Portage, Westbourne and North-Western (now the Manitoba and North-Western) Railway branched off from the Canadian Pacific Railway at Portage la Prairie, and took its way over the northwestern part of the Province, heading for Prince Albert on the North Saskatchewan. From this road, in turn, there was built last year, beginning at Gladstone, the Lake Dauphin Railway, which strikes northward to the fertile areas in the direction of Lake Dauphin and Lake Winnipegosis, and which may become a route to the northern seaboard. Down through the beautiful districts of south-western Manitoba two lines of railway run from Winnipeg, tapping one of the richest grain districts of the West, also the soft coal deposits of the Estevan region; while north and north-westward short branches run to Stonewall and Selkirk. From the south the Northern Pacific Railway (the first to enter the field as a rival of the Canadian Pacific Railway) and the Great Northern Railway enter through the States, and over the road of the former the Grand Trunk Railway, eager for its share of western trade, is now running special colonist trains into Winnipeg. The Northern Pacific has also pushed westward, by two branches from Winnipeg, to Brandon and Portage la Prairie respectively. From Chater, on the Canadian Pacific Railway, the North-West Central Railway goes northward to Hamiota. Away out on its line towards the coast the Canadian Pacific Railway sends out offshoots in many directions. From Brandon a line runs south into the Souris district; from Regina a line goes to Prince Albert; from Calgary one strikes north-westward through the Red Deer country to Edmonton. Southward from the great transcontinental road a branch runs from Medicine Hat to the coal mines at Lethbridge, and from Calgary through the vast ranching country to Fort Macleod; while out in the rich mining districts of British Columbia branches tap every centre of any importance. For a long time the question of railway communication from the west to the east and south was a burning one in our politics, and as one charter after another passed by the Local Legislature in Manitoba was disallowed by the Dominion authorities, on the ground that the Canadian Pacific Railway, while still struggling, would suffer, feeling in the West rose sometimes to fever pitch. It was largely through a fruitless fighting on behalf of Provincial rights in this matter that the Norquay Government fell, but since the time when, shortly after the Greenway Administration took office, the Northern Pacific Railway entered the Province, we have had, as I have shown, railroads numerous enough. There are more to follow, and the change wrought in the course of a few years makes a marvellous contrast between the isolation of the early days and our present closeness of contact with all the great centres on the continent.

CHAPTER IX.

A "BOOM" AND ANOTHER REBELLION.

ONCE communication with the outside world was established, the growth of the country's life in all lines was comparatively rapid. We say "comparatively" in view of its former isolation, but there has never been what in western phrase would be called "a stampede" of immigration towards this country as compared with the influx of population other new lands have sometimes received. For that reason it is claimed that the conditions of life and work which now obtain in the West are much more solid and substantial than might be expected from the age of its history, inasmuch as the population came in so gradually that it has been readily assimilated and made part and parcel of the institutions of the land.

But though there has never been for any protracted period a rush into this country, our history is not altogether destitute of that

HON. THOMAS GREENWAY,
Premier of Manitoba.

adjunct to the progress of all young territories known as a "boom" time. That particular epoch came upon the West in the fall and winter of 1882-83. Just what began it we cannot say, except that there was general prosperity at that time in many parts of the world, and that capital looking for investment found its way to the new land whose resources were beginning to compel attention from without.

The "boom" opened in the fall of 1882, with the turning over of a few lots in Winnipeg, but as they went on turning over at considerable advance in price, men plunged wildly in, and the young city became in a few weeks a seething sea of real estate brokers, speculators and auctioneers. The auctioneers' rooms were a sight to see, as some man with "the dangerous gift of fluency" flourished a pointer with which he indicated the choice lots on a map, and expatiated on the merits of some coming Chicago to the men who clambered over each other in haste to buy. Fortunes were made and lost in a few days' time, figures became meaningless of real value, and we have known men without any available money make ten thousand dollars in a single evening. Fabulous prices were paid for all sorts of real estate, and "towns" with the slightest possible chance for the future commanded for their corner lots large figures, while places long leagues from railway communication were readily sold on the off chance of some railroad heading that way.

Great harm was done to the country by all this "wild-cat" speculation. The people themselves got inflated ideas and extravagant habits which they afterwards tried with disastrous results to maintain after the means to do so had been exhausted. The effect outside told terribly against the country. The many in different parts of the world who were "bitten" turned against the West, and denounced everything connected with it as a swindle and fraud. They themselves were to blame for the haste to be rich that impelled them to make investments ignorantly, but the specious accounts given them by the "land sharks" were set down against the country. When on a mission field in southern Manitoba, in 1890, one of my people received from a lady school-teacher in Ireland a sum of money to pay her taxes on town lots in a place called Pomeroy, and she asked on what street a certain family lived, and would he kindly send her a copy of the Pomeroy paper. At that date, Pomeroy consisted (as it still does) of a farm-house and a lot of surveyors' stakes on the virgin prairie, and there was no newspaper published within fifteen miles of it. This state of matters was gently hinted to the Irish school-teacher, with the result that she, like many others similarly situated, became the reverse of an emigration agent for Manitoba. But the "boom" drew widespread attention to the country, and scattered people far and wide over it, westward towards the Rocky Mountains, and north-westward along the valleys of the great Saskatchewan. New territories with ever-growing autonomy were carved out on the prairies, with central points such as Regina, Calgary, Edmonton, Prince Albert, Battleford and other now thriving communities.

When Canada first took over the great North-West Territory, only a corner out of its vast area had been organized into a province, and called Manitoba; but in 1872 an Act was passed in Ottawa providing for the government of the unorganized territory by the Lieutenant-Governor of Manitoba and a council appointed by the federal authorities.

The members of this first Council, gazetted in January, 1873, are herewith given: Hons. M. A. Girard, Donald A. Smith, Henry J. Clarke, Patrice Breland, Alfred Boyd, John Schultz, Joseph Dubuc, A. G. B. Bannatyne, William Fraser, Robert Hamilton and William Christie.

To these were afterwards added: Hons. James McKay, Joseph Royal, Pierre Delorme, W. R. Bown, W. N. Kennedy, John H. McTavish and William Tait. This Council, presided over by Lieutenant-Governor Morris, of Manitoba, did exceedingly important service in trying times, and paved the way for fuller organization.

Acts were shortly afterwards passed by the Dominion Parliament, establishing the Mounted Police force and making rules for the regulation of trade, notably for the suppression of liquor selling, the Territories being put practically under prohibition, in order to keep liquor out of the reach of the inflammable and easily excited Indian population. Treaties had been made with the Indians far and wide, and such was the fairness with which the Government treated them, and such was the influence of the Mounted Police, that when the Custer massacre and similar events were taking place south of the boundary, on the north all was peace and comparative quietness.

In 1875 an Act for the fuller organization and government of the North-West Territories was introduced by the Hon. Alex. Mackenzie, and came into force in October, 1876, the Hon. David Laird being appointed the first lieutenant-governor, aided by a small Council consisting of Stipendiary Magistrates McLeod, Ryan, Richardson and Major Irvine (N.-W. M. P.), A. E. Forget, Secretary of the Council; M. St. John, Sheriff. The position of Governor Laird and his Council was not an easy one, as the changing conditions, the disappearance of the buffalo

HON. EDGAR DEWDNEY.

and other means of support, were throwing upon the Governor the burden of caring for and arranging about the future of almost the entire native population of Indians and half-breeds.

Gov. Laird was succeeded in the governorship by Hon. Edgar Dewdney, in 1881. The Territories were divided into local electoral districts, with a legislative assembly meeting at Regina, and into Dominion constituencies, with the privilege of sending four members to the House of Commons. The whole territory was divided into judicial districts, with experienced and able jurists at the head of each; and the vast domain was becoming the prosperous home of thousands when a second rebellion broke out in 1885, and for a time checked the progress by disturbing the peace of the land.

Just what gave rise to the North-West rebellion is perhaps more than anyone can definitely say. Political gladiators have fought the question over and over again to no definite end, and probably the great parties have their own opinion in the matter to this day, though they may be chary about telling all they know. It appears certain that the French half-breeds who were settled on the south branch of the Saskatchewan River (many of them being the same, or of the same, families as those concerned in the Riel rebellion of '69) were determined to hold to the old system of long narrow farms fronting on the river, as against the rectangular, or "square," survey proposed by the Government, which threatened to break up the homes they had built and overturn the old social life fostered by contiguous residence; and it seems also tolerably clear that many of the settlers had been waiting an extraordinarily long time for their land patents and scrip. These things were sufficient to unsettle the easily ruffled and somewhat turbulent half-breed element, and once anything like rebellion was contemplated, the aid of their duskier brethren all over the great plains was confidently expected.

The local authorities seem to have been singularly oblivious of the excitement that was afoot, and of the meetings that were being held for the redress of the wrongs alleged. They do not seem to have kept those at the seat of federal government properly informed as to the true state of matters at the scene of the discontent, nor of the important fact that many of the white settlers in the region sympathized with the malcontents at the outset, though deprecating the use of any but constitutional means for redress. But it is doubtful whether the discontent that seethed under the surface would ever have burst into active rebellion had not the agitators sent for Louis Riel, who since his first escapade had been living in the United States, and who at the time he was sent for was engaged in the quiet work of school-teaching in Montana. The malcontents felt that, with his energetic personality at their head, they could secure all the rights they claimed, and so despatched a deputation asking him to come and lead them in their struggle. The reply of Riel was exceedingly characteristic of the man, being a mixture of the egotist, the mercenary and the patriot, and in June, 1884, he accompanied the deputation back to the North-West. The very presence of the man on the ground should have put the local authorities on the alert. But either the local powers were making light of the situation, or else the pigeon-holes at Ottawa were receiving unread petitions, and so far as we can gather, we incline to the former as the more correct opinion. Then as anyone who knew Riel should have expected, the inevitable sequel came. He was a man easily excited and inordinately vain; hence, as he felt the wine of a new movement in his system, and became intoxicated with the success of his fiery appeals to the meetings that assembled, he broke out into amazing and extravagant pretensions. He openly separated from the Church of Rome, and such was his influence over the French half-breeds that he drew them from allegiance to their priests. He added David to his name, and called himself "Louis David Riel exovede," in allusion to both his kingly and his priestly claims; he established a Government with headquarters at Batoche, arrested whom he pleased, plundered the stores around, and sent word to Major Crozier, who commanded the Mounted Police at Fort Carlton, the nearest post, to surrender at once. This was rushing matters with a vengeance, and it is not surprising that, on the 19th of March, Major Crozier, hearing of these things, sent word to Prince Albert for help, and shortly afterwards despatched Thomas McKay, one of the Prince Albert volunteers, to remonstrate with Riel.

The McKay family did signal service for the country during the rebellion, there being no less than five brothers of them engaged in its suppression. Being natives of the country they were thoroughly at home in camp or in saddle, were deadly shots, had immense endurance and unmistakable courage. One of them, George, a canon in the Anglican Church, accompanied our column as chaplain and scout, and I can vouch for it that he could fight as well as pray.

When Thomas McKay reached Riel's Council at Batoche, he found things at white heat, and was told by Riel that there was to be a war of extermination during which " the two curses, the Government and the Hudson's Bay Company," and all who sympathized with them, were to be driven out of the country. "You don't know what we are after," said Riel to McKay. "We want blood, blood—it's blood we want." McKay, barely escaping with his life from such a gory atmosphere, returned to Carlton, and the next day, in company with Mitchell, of Duck Lake, met Nolin and Maxime Lepine (brother of Ambroise Lepine, Riel's adjutant in '69-'70), from Riel, demanding the surrender of Fort Carlton. This, of course, was refused, and in a few days rebellion was rampant with a madman at its head.

For many weeks previous Riel had been sending his runners amongst the Indians, and counted on a general uprising of the tribes, assuring them that the Government could easily be overthrown and that the whole country would be theirs again. We can forgive Riel for a good many things, but to justify his incitement of the Indians to murder and rapine is more than any reasonable person cares to undertake. As a rule the Indians were perfectly satisfied on the splendid reserves the Government had provided for them, were well cared for and taught, but the savage instinct was still strong in them, and to let them loose on defenceless homes with all the horrors of the scalping-knife and the torture, seems to take the man

who is responsible for it out of the reach of
ordinary consideration, and puts a tongue in
every wound of the massacred calling for
justice on the foul compasser of their death.

The first actual collision took place near Duck
Lake, on March 26th, when Crozier, in an effort
to secure stores from that point, met Gabriel
Dumont, the redoubtable fighter, in command of
a large force of half-breeds and Indians. A flag
of truce was displayed by Dumont's party, but
while parleying with the leaders Crozier saw
that the rebels were surrounding his force of
police and Prince Albert volunteers, and he immediately gave the order to fire. He, however,
was directly in front, and his men held the fire
of their 9-pounder on that account, though the
gallant officer told them afterwards that they
should have obeyed orders and shot him, if need
be, with the enemy.

Firing became general, and after an hour
Crozier and his men, who had acted throughout
with the utmost coolness, were forced to retire
before superior numbers, leaving twelve dead
on the field and taking with them twenty-five
wounded. They arrived at Fort Carlton, where
they were joined two days afterwards by Col.
Irvine, with eighty police and thirty more
volunteers from plucky Prince Albert, and as

there was no advantage in holding Fort Carlton, they retired from it to Prince Albert, where the greater portion of them remained till the close of the rebellion.

For this inaction the Mounted Police, than whom no more gallant force exists in the world, have been much criticised by ignorant people; but those who know that without them the most populous community in that part of the West would have been at the mercy of the now savage and excited enemy, honor the brave men who repressed their desire to be at the front, and loyally did less brilliant but not less important duty in defending the otherwise defenceless homes of the district.

Gabriel Dumont was certainly the most striking figure amongst the rebels in all the fighting which followed the battle at Duck Lake. He was living quietly enough upon his farm on the South Saskatchewan when the agitation began, but from his noted prowess and activity in the conflicts and hunts on the great plains in former years, became at once the acknowledged military leader of the rebel force. He was a man of magnificent physique and vast strength, a daring rider, a deadly shot, and, withal, possessed of undoubted dash and courage. It is not generally known that he

GABRIEL DUMONT,

Leader of rebel forces in second Riel Rebellion, 1885.

was wounded at Duck Lake by a bullet which plowed along his scalp and felled him, stunned and bleeding, to the ground. There are some who say that after that experience he was more cautious about exposing himself. The incident, however, could not have materially affected his nerve, for it is well known to some that but for the interference of Riel he would, on a night of cold and rain, have led a "forlorn hope" in a midnight raid on Middleton's camp just before the fight at Fish Creek. How that raid would have eventuated it is useless to conjecture, but one who has passed nights in such a camp on such a night could easily see what confusion would be caused by a rush that would stampede the horses and produce a momentary panic. From their bearing in all situations during the campaign, we know that our boys would have been equal to the occasion; but from the rebel standpoint Dumont's proposition stamps him as a man of courage as well as of considerable strategic ability.*

The news of the disaster at Duck Lake sped like a flash to the hearts of the Canadian people, and the one thing of value that resulted from

---

* No proceedings were ever taken against Dumont. He left the country for a time after the rebellion, but is now a peaceful resident.

this wretched rebellion was the manner in which the spontaneous rush to arms manifested the spirit of the nation. Procrastinating officialdom had had its day. A Commission, consisting of Messrs. W. P. R. Street, A. E. Forget and Roger Goulet, was appointed, on the 30th March, to investigate the claims of the half-breeds, and when the Government, who never before seemed to be fully seized of the situation, started in vigorously to suppress the uprising, they found the people of all parties more than ready to second their efforts. The alertness with which the people answered the bugle's call to arms reminds one of the incident related by Scott in "The Lady of the Lake," when in answer to the shrill whistle of Roderick Dhu the sides of Ben Ledi swarmed with Highland clansmen, as

"Every tuft of broom gave life
To plaided warrior armed for strife."

Scarcely had the story of Duck Lake reached the seat of Government at Ottawa, when from the frowning fortress of old Quebec to Halifax away down by the sea, from the populous cities and backwoods farms of Ontario to the scattered ranches at the foot-hills of the Rocky Mountains, hosts of armed men sprang up to defend the laws and liberties of the land they loved. As we look into the situation we do not wonder at this swift response to the country's call. There was something peculiarly touching and pathetic about the death on that ill-fated field of the young men from Prince Albert who had gone outside the ordinary routine of their life to help the authorities maintain order in the country. A friend in Prince Albert said to me, on the way back after the rebellion was over, "If one had picked out the men we could least afford to spare from the community, he would certainly have included the nine who were killed at Duck Lake." And so as the people of Canada heard of those who fell in the prime and glory of their young manhood, and thought that far away from their homes and the peaceful graves of their fathers they were sleeping their last long sleep, wrapped in the snow-shroud of the western prairies, and that, instead of the accents of those they loved, the last sounds that had fallen upon their ears were the mad rattle of the rifle and the fierce yellings of a treacherous foe, we are not surprised that a great wave of mingled sorrow and wrath swept over the country.

To these feelings that humanity would dictate add those of patriotism and national pride, and it is little marvel that when the uniform of the Queen was fired upon there was a mighty and immediate answer to the country's call. For sixty long years now the Queen has swayed a gracious and commanding sceptre over an empire so vast "that the beat of her morning drum, following the sun and keeping company with the hours, encircles the globe with one continuous strain of the martial airs of England." Over all this vast domain the story of the Queen's life has become one of the prized possessions of her subjects. Her career, so strangely chequered with joy and sorrow, has brought out perfect types of girlhood, wifehood and motherhood, while her strong common-sense has so linked her to the love and esteem of her people, that we can say in truth of her what Edmund Burke so vainly hoped for Marie Antoinette when he said: "I thought ten thousand swords must have leaped from their scabbards to avenge even a look that threatened her with insult."

Hence we find the most strenuous action at once taken by the Government, who without delay sent forward General Middleton, the commander-in-chief of the Canadian forces, to take swift measures for the suppression of the rebellion.

General Middleton was a man of many battlefields, and though the North-West Rebellion provided new experience in a peculiar warfare, he bore himself throughout as a man of the utmost coolness and courage—in short, a true British soldier of the best type.

He arrived in Winnipeg on the 27th of

LIEUT.-COL. OSBORNE SMITH.

March, and left that same night for the scene with the 90th Rifles and the Winnipeg Field Battery. Troops from all parts of Canada, to the number of five or six thousand, were hurrying to the front, and in the West every district was furnishing a ready quota to the various bodies being raised for the occasion. Winnipeg and the Province of Manitoba, besides the battery, cavalry and Boulton's scouts, furnished three infantry regiments, two of them, the 91st, under Col. Scott, and the 92nd (Winnipeg Light Infantry), under Col. Osborne Smith, being specially enlisted in a few days for the suppression of the rebellion. With the latter regiment I had the honor to serve, and I purpose giving some personal recollections of the campaign such as have apparently been interesting to Canadian audiences at many points.

As indicated in the preface to this book, no attempt is made to give a complete record of the military operations of the whole force in the field. One can only be in one place at a time, and this volume is chiefly one of personal reminiscence; but it is hoped that the account here given, as written out from notes made nightly at the camp-fire, will be in some measure typical of the experience of all who went to the front.

NORTH-WEST LEGISLATIVE ASSEMBLY, 1886.

1. Lieut. Governor Dewdney.
2. Judge Richardson.
3. Judge Rouleau.
4. John G. Turriff
5. H yter Reed.
6. H S. Cayley.
7. Robert Crawford.
8. James Ross.
9. David F. Jelly.
10. Major Irvine.
11. J. G. Secord.
12. J. D. Lauder.
13. Senator Perley.
14. Chas. Marshallsay.
15. Owen E. Hughes.
16. Sam. Cunningham.
17. A. E. Forget.
18. Jimmie McArn (first page of the House).
N. Lord Boyle.

CHAPTER X.

CAMPAIGNING ON THE PRAIRIES.

THE regiment known as the Winnipeg Light Infantry may be spoken of as one recruited out of almost every nation under heaven. The main body of it was made up of men enlisted in the city of Winnipeg, to which the noise of tumult had brought adventurers from every point of the compass, many of whom hailed the rebellion as a great windfall. Numbers of men just back from the Gordon Relief Expedition up the Nile fell readily into the ranks. Some of Indian, Irish, Scotch, English, Icelandic, German, French, and I know not what other extraction, were on hand, and I remember two men who followed our company to quarters one day and forswore their allegiance to the United States—till the close of the campaign, when, with four months' pay in their pockets, they shook the dust of Canada off their feet and returned to Chicago. One company, however, was enlisted in the old pioneer parish of Kildonan and contiguous points, from the farmers there, and another was enrolled from Minnedosa, a point some 150 miles distant to the north-west of the city. To the Kildonan company (afterwards No. 1 in the regiment) I, who was a native of the parish and at that time a student-at-law in Winnipeg, attached myself as a full private, though in the process of unaccountable events, and to my own great surprise, I became shortly afterwards second lieutenant.

It was significant of the times that our company had its barracks in a deserted "boom" house, whose hardwood floors made an excellent place for drill. After some scant preliminary training we left Kildonan, suitably farewelled, on the 13th of April, to join our regiment in the city. As we marched up, one of those incidents common in the experience of amateur soldiers occurred in passing the camp of the 9th Voltigeurs of Quebec. The guard turned out and presented arms, but we did not know how to return the compliment, and so kept on steadily as if they had not attracted our attention. Fortunately, however, we happened to be marching "at the shoulder," and I suppose that to this day the 9th have no idea that it was only by the merest chance in the world we did the right thing at the right time.

On Wednesday, the 15th, after being addressed by Lieutenant-Governor Aikins, our regiment marched to the C. P. R. station, and it was then known that we were under orders for the extreme north-west of the Territories, where the Frog Lake massacre had just taken place, and where the posts and settlements on the North Saskatchewan were in danger from the surrounding Indians. Soon the final farewells were said—for how long we knew not—and with many a last word and handclasp the severest ordeal of all was over, and the train moved out amidst the answering cheers of those going away and those left behind.

Doubtless many a stalwart uniformed figure was held in more than necessary military erectness, and many a voice firm enough in command was hushed lest a tell-tale tremor should reveal to others the sorrow felt at seeing lost in the heaving throng some dear and well-known face. But such feelings, however deep and constant, must be kept in check—soldiers, we thought, must be made of sterner stuff—and so before we had travelled many miles the usual gaiety of spirits, the amusing story and the patriotic song were in evidence, and no grim forebodings were allowed to displace the enjoyment of the hour.

The car in which No. 1 (Kildonan) Company

travelled was certainly a jovial one, and a good deal of the mirth was at the expense of the guard at the door, a man who had been enlisted at the last moment from some outside point, when he was barely recovered from a prolonged spree, and who made grotesque efforts to spring to sober attention whenever the officer of the night passed through to see that all was well. The judgment of our color-sergeant, at whose request the man was enrolled, was amply vindicated during the campaign, for the wild-looking soldier of that first night, once beyond the reach of liquor, became one of the finest marchers in the regiment, and the head navigator for our flat-boat flotilla on the North Saskatchewan.

Our flying special "halted" at 11 a.m. of the next day at the town of Moose Jaw for breakfast, and the fast from the previous afternoon, together with the knowledge that we would soon be beyond the reach of what is ordinarily called a "square meal," led to such display of appetite that, when the regiment boarded the train, Moose Jaw must have somewhat resembled a country just traversed by an army of locusts.

Our next stop was at Gleichen, or Crowfoot Crossing, near the home of Crowfoot, the redoubtable chief of the Blackfoot Indians, whose reserve was near at hand. Crowfoot promised to be loyal, and he kept his word; but as the spirit of rebellion was abroad at the time, and young braves are easily roused, the Minnedosa Company was left here to repress any undue exuberance. We saw Crowfoot several times going to and from Calgary, a stern, stoical man,

CROWFOOT.
(From photograph by Prof. Buell.)

whose will was law for his tribe, and whose consistent loyalty was of great value to Canada during that troublous time.

To Calgary we came on the 17th of April, amid a drizzling rain and snow, but after the first night the weather, which Calgarians assured us was exceptional, cleared and was beautiful during the remainder of our stay. Some of the prophecies made concerning Calgary have not yet come true, but it is, nevertheless, one of the most perfect sites for a city in the west. We shall not soon forget the view from the great mound across the Elbow River in those spring evenings. The town, on its picturesque upland, lay peacefully quiet at the close of the day. Around it twined the glistening coils of the Bow and the Elbow rivers, which pour their united waters into the great Saskatchewan, while away to the west the Rockies, mighty monuments of the Creator's power, reared their snowy peaks against the purpling sky, resembling the vast tents of some giant host rising majestically above the plain.

Calgary, on its more material side, seemed that year the very paradise of cowboys, horsemen and scouts, for the place was full of the great rough, good-hearted fellows, fairly bristling with arms. Belts of cartridges round the waist and slashed across the chest held supplies for the Winchester rifle and Colt's revolver; great leather leggings, called "schaps," bowie-knives here and there about the person, huge jingling spurs, immense grey hats turned up at one side, "the cavalry swagger," and somewhat ferocious language were the prevailing characteristics. These men were magnificent riders, more at home in the saddle than on carpets, and as they had the run of the town, the sight of a number of them, with their wild horses at full speed along the principal streets, was quite common.

Most of us who had been brought up in the West knew something by experience of bronchobreaking, but it was worth while going to the corrals to see the broncho broken for use in our column. The horse, perhaps five or six years old, had never been handled except to be branded when a foal. He was dexterously lassoed, and (as the whole process is one of breaking rather than training) if necessary choked into submission. Sometimes the headstall was fastened with a blindfold, the great saddle was thrown on and tightly "cinched," then a cowboy leaped into the seat, locked his spurs and yelled " Let her loose!" There was a scattering of those holding the broncho, and a retrograde movement quickly executed on the part of the spectators as the trouble began. Sometimes the broncho, dazed for a few moments, stood with hunched-up back or walked quietly away for a few yards, then suddenly "exploded" into the air with terrific violence, and came down facing the opposite direction, with a continuation of such "bucking" as only a well-regulated broncho understands. The rider, however, was generally what westerners call a "stayer," and after a half-hour or so the broncho gave up and was pronounced "broken"; but we would not advise any of our tender-foot friends to mount the "hurricane deck" of a broncho, even though he may be broken enough for a cowboy's use.

Orders shortly came that our column was to march northward to the relief of Edmonton and the districts on the North Saskatchewan, which were being terrorized by Big Bear and his tribe, a portion of whom had massacred nine men at Frog Lake on the 2nd of April. Word, too, had just reached us of the fight at Fish Creek between Middleton and Riel, with heavy loss to our comrades.

The Fish Creek fight was evidently planned by Gabriel Dumont as a surprise for our troops, and it certainly did come upon them with unexpected suddenness. It would be utterly wrong to say, as some have said, that Middleton walked into a trap, for he had his mounted infantry and Boulton's scouts well spread out in front in proper form. But men who were in the advance guard of the 90th have told me that the first indication of the enemy's presence they had was in seeing several of the scouts in front fall from their saddles under the deadly fire of the half-breeds concealed in the bluffs. The main body of the volunteers was soon brought up to support the scouts, and the fighting became general. A ravine near by afforded almost perfect cover to the enemy, and from it a hot fusilade was poured upon the advancing troops. Dumont's men also set the prairie on fire so that the smoke would confuse the volunteers, but they put out the fire and advanced steadily, adopting the enemy's tactics and taking cover as much as possible. After some hours the half-breeds, except a few in the ravine, were dislodged from their position, and as a heavy thunderstorm was beginning Middleton decided to form camp for the night. In this fight eleven of our men were killed or died subsequently of wounds, and a large number were wounded more or less seriously. When this news reached us at Calgary, just as we were under orders for the north, our letters home probably took on a final farewell flavor, and, withal, contained bequests of our worldly goods as holograph wills.

When we marched out towards Edmonton on the afternoon of the 27th we had but 165 men of our own regiment, the rest being on detachment duty, but we had two small bodies of Mounted Police and scouts under command of Major Steele, Major Hatton and

Capt. Oswald. About six miles out we crossed the Bow River by fording, and this was one of the first of many picturesque scenes on our route. The river was wide and swift-flowing, the water where we crossed on the stony bottom being from two to four feet deep. The loaded wagons, with four and six horses or mules driven by skilful though somewhat profane teamsters, the red-coated soldiers, the Mounted Police in scarlet and gold, and the picturesque corps of scouts, all passing through the water together, made a view worthy of being placed on canvas. Occasionally the scene would be spoiled by a mule throwing himself down in the water, but the free use of the black-snake whip, with the freer use of language not to be repeated here, overcame the obstinacy of the animal. A few miles farther out we camped for the night. A marvellously beautiful night it was, and I shall not soon forget how still and white the encampment looked under the splendor of the moon as it shone upon the tents grouped together on the wide prairie. It was probably on such a night that the young shepherd watching his flocks on the uplands of Canaan saw the infinite stairways of stardust that "sloped through darkness up to God," and exclaimed, "When I consider the heavens, the work of thy fingers, the moon and the stars which thou hast ordained, what is man that thou art mindful of him, or the son of man that thou visitest him?" Few men remain wholly unmoved under a study of the starry heavens, and doubtless many a sentry beneath those eloquent skies night after night drank in new messages as to the sublimity and goodness of God.

The next morning the strident notes of the bugle-band sounded *reveille* at half-past four, and breaking camp early we marched twenty-five miles our first day. On we went with the usual round of marching by day and guard by night till we came to the Red Deer River, where, it being high-water time, we were stopped by what Adjutant Constantine (now in command of the Mounted Police in the Yukon country) called "a wide, swift-flowing and treacherous stream." After many futile attempts a rude ferry was constructed, upon which, under the pilotage of Sergt. Pritchard, of No. 1 Company, we all crossed in safety, and set out on our march of 110 miles to Edmonton.

On May 7th we came upon the first bands of Indians, numerous enough and of the Cree tribe, under chiefs bearing the not very classical names of Ermine-Skin, Cayoté, and Bobtail.

Whether these were disposed to be hostile or not we did not know, but our Colonel held the men in readiness for any event; and then, with bayonets fixed and rifles at the slope, with band playing and every weapon exposed to view, we marched through, while the Indians gathered in

INTERIOR OF H. B. CO.'S FORT AT EDMONTON.

the woods by the roadside and gazed wonderingly at the spectacle.

We reached Edmonton on May 8th, and encamped south of the town in the midst of wigwams. The Indians were loyal enough now, with flags displayed from the tepees, in the presence of an armed force; but the Edmonton people gratefully assured us that only the

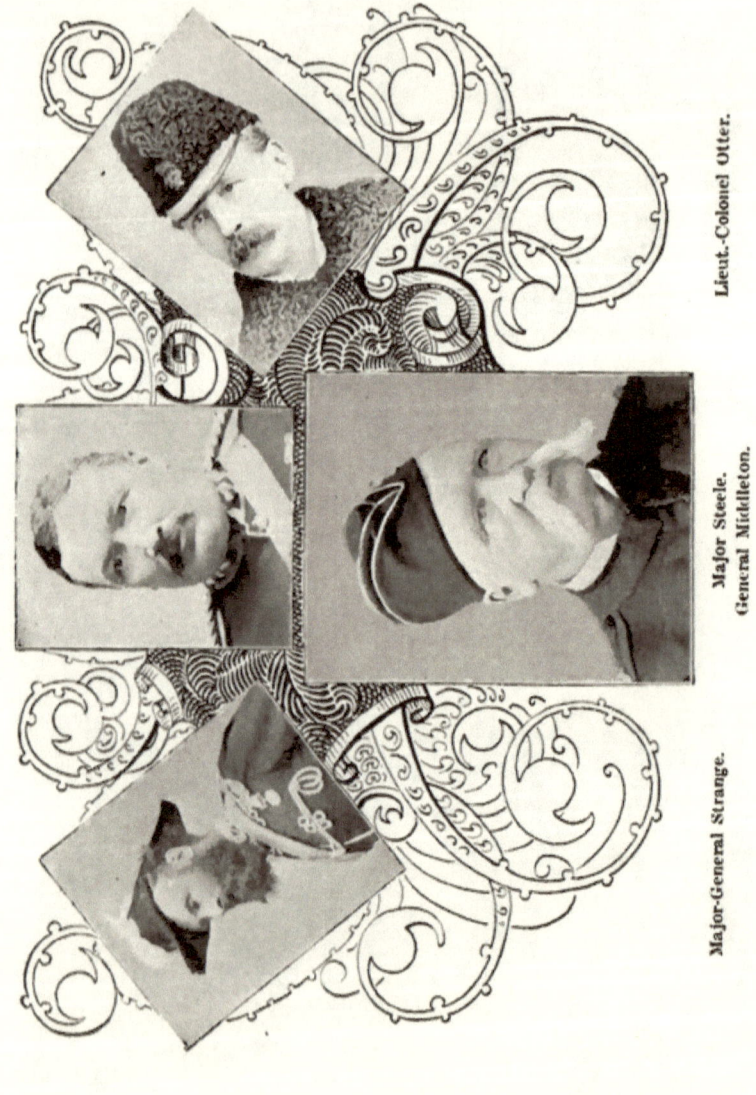

Lieut.-Colonel Otter. Major Steele. General Middleton. Major-General Strange.

timely arrival of our column had prevented
repetitions of the Frog Lake massacre at many
points along the North Saskatchewan. At
Edmonton we met the commander of our
brigade, General Strange, who with part of that
plucky regiment, the 65th of Montreal, and a
detachment of Mounted Police under Major
Perry, had preceded us a few days. General
Strange was a retired British army officer, who
was living on a ranch near Calgary when the
rebellion broke out, and was given command of
our column. He had done signal and distinguished service as an officer of artillery in the
Indian mutiny and elsewhere, and in every
respect was a splendid type of the British
soldier. Somewhat eccentric in certain ways,
he was, withal, as kindly of heart as he was
brusque of manner, and so cool and courageous
that by the end of the campaign every man in
the column had personal affection for him, and
would have gone at his command wherever
men could go. On this occasion, at Edmonton,
General Strange made a speech complimenting
the men highly on the swift march they had
made. The speech was delivered in characteristic soldier style, with few words, and these
shot out with quick emphasis, like the firing of
bullets. As we crossed the ferry and marched

into Edmonton, we saw the picturesque town, with its Hudson's Bay post, the great distributing point for the Company's fur-trade, rising high on the north bank of the North Saskatchewan, and stretching out over considerable territory. Edmonton had borne its part in the "boom," and was mainly responsible for the breaking of it, as some men, coming to themselves, realized how foolish they had been to buy lots at an enormous figure in a place, at that date, 210 miles from even a prospective railway station (though it is now connected by rail with the C.P.R. from Calgary).

We remained at Edmonton a few days while flat-boats were being made to take us down the river, and I especially remember that with the lavish hand of the soldier of Epicurean philosophy, we spent our scanty cash in buying up the ancient stock of delicacies (?) from the Hudson's Bay store. Dried apples and prunes, ginger bread of rocky firmness, canned fruit, and such like, found their way to our tents, and on these unaccustomed delicacies we fared sumptuously for several days. On the 14th of May we embarked in open flat-boats to go down the river, greatly to the dismay of our Edmonton friends, who asserted that the Indians would enjoy the sport of standing on the high banks

and "potting" us as we went by. Well do I
remember the first night out, when our flat-
boats were tied to trees and we encamped in
a storm, half rain, half snow, for the night, for
I was officer in command of the picket. The
twenty-five men fell in as best they could to
be inspected in the darkness and on the sliding
mud of the bank. Then we groped our way
through the wet bush some distance to the rear
of the camp, where we posted our line of sentries,
while the rest of the picket huddled together
under the dripping trees. The work of relieving
sentries was made difficult by the very darkness
of the forest; but the slightest movement drew
out the hoarse challenge, and the sentry thus
found always gladly welcomed the relief. At
four o'clock we came in, roused the camp, got
on board breakfastless, and moved down the
river in a driving snow-storm, with our clothes
standing upon us like icy coats of mail. On
the 16th we landed at Fort Victoria, which had
been recently looted by Big Bear and his band,
who were now sullenly retreating before us with
all the prisoners and their ill-gotten plunder.

On Sunday, the 17th, we had three church
services. In the morning Col. Smith, assisted
by Adjt. Constantine and Surgeon Pennyfather,
read the Church of England service, with the

big drum for a pulpit; in the afternoon the well-known Methodist minister, the Rev. John McDougall, of Morley, who was with our column, preached in a long building near by; while Mr. Mackenzie, the Presbyterian chaplain to the Mounted Police, became a "field preacher," and conducted service in the woods in the evening.

Reference already has been made to the amateur drill witnessed on such an expedition as this, and an incident that occurred at the close of the morning service was, I fear, more discussed and made more impression than the service itself. It being the official church parade, the whole regiment was formed up in three sides of a square, facing in to the "pulpit." When service was over the Colonel turned the parade over for dismissal to another member of the staff. This officer faced the situation, and knew just enough about drill to know that he should get the men back into line before giving the "dismiss," but how to get them there in military order was more than he could tell for the life of him. But he was a man of resource, and boldly went at it. "Regiment! 'Tion! Men on the sides, backwards wheel." They, however, had never heard such an order before and had never practised circus drill, so they remained motionless till Sergt.-Major (now Capt.) Lawlor, a Crimean veteran, who often had to unravel tangles during our campaign, came to the rescue and dismissed the parade in the orthodox way.

While at Fort Victoria, in "the enemy's country," orders had been issued that no man should leave the camp; but failing to understand the full purport of this, a soldier who was an ardent disciple of Izaak Walton got an old punt and pushed across the river to a likely-looking creek to do some fishing. His return was witnessed by the Colonel, who happened to be on the bank, and that officer immediately sent the sergeant of the guard (Sutherland, of No. 1 Company) to arrest and bring the man before him. To Sutherland's surprise the "outlaw" proved to be Pritchard, one of his fellow-sergeants in No. 1, who submitted good-humoredly to the arrest, but insisted on bringing his string of fish with him. The Colonel was equally surprised, Pritchard being a favorite all round, and the very opposite of a wilful offender; but as the sergeant had been of prime service to the column in crossing the Red Deer River, and as he moreover gravely avowed that he had been intending the best fish for the Colonel's dinner, that officer, keeping his face straight with great difficulty, administered a reprimand and set the offender at liberty.

On May the 20th we left Fort Victoria on our march overland after Big Bear, who had "looted" all the posts between Edmonton and Battleford, and at Fort Pitt, near the scene of the Frog Lake massacre, had received the surrender of Mr. W. J. McLean, the Hudson's Bay officer in charge, together with all his family and employees, whom he now held as prisoners. To secure the release of these prisoners and to break up the armed force of the Indians became now the objects of our expedition, and as the sequel showed, both these objects were accomplished, happily without much immediate loss of life.

Various points northward were passed, such as Saddle Lake (where some of the atrocities had been committed, the leader in which, a giant Indian named Mamanook, was shot with some others by Steele's scouts a few days after this), Egg Lake and Dog Rump Creek, not far from Frog Lake. During these days the rain fell almost incessantly; it was a case of marching in the mud by day and sleeping in our wet clothes by night. To make matters worse, our commissariat was not well supplied, and until further supplies, which were being brought from Edmonton, would reach us, we were on half rations. It was an uncomfortable predicament to be in, and I remember standing by a campfire which the rain was like to extinguish, and distinctly envying two scouts who were enjoying a repast of "hard tack" and black tea after a day of hard riding.

On May 23rd, after a long day's march, we had orders to camp on the low ground beneath a ridge to avoid advertising our presence to the Indians, but the place was a shaking bog, and after a few vain attempts to prevent the tent-poles and pegs from going through towards the antipodes, Surgeon Pennyfather refused to risk the health of the men by asking them to sleep there, and preferred rightly to have them risk their lives as targets on the ridge, where we accordingly encamped.

On the following morning *reveille* sounded as usual at 4.30, and we rose from our cheerless bivouacs on the muddy ground. At 5.10 we fell in amidst drenching rain and driving wind, and were addressed by General Strange as follows:

" Col. Osborne Smith, officers and men of the Winnipeg Light Infantry, you have marched well. I know that you will stick to me, and we will stick to Big Bear's trail as long as our grub lasts. This is the Queen's birthday; we have no time to celebrate and can't have fireworks, but let us hope we soon will have fireworks with the enemy. Boys, three cheers for the Queen; God bless her!"

To my mind no incident during the campaign more amply demonstrated the loyal hearts of our boys. It is easy to make a fair showing and to feel enthusiasm on the parade ground amidst a cheering throng of spectators, but the environment of our boys was different that morning. They were away out on the hillside in the solitary wilderness, rain-drenched in the driving storm, but at the name of the Queen they stood in the ranks with heads uncovered, and when the old General called for cheers the shout that went up might well have rent the concave of the low-hanging clouds. Then the General, who with all his bluff exterior was an earnest Christian, said:

"Boys, this is also Sunday, but we have no time for service to-day; we must push on the march. I am reminded of an old soldier, who on going into battle prayed, 'O God, I often forget thee. I will be very busy to-day. I am sure to forget thee, but do not forget me.' Boys, we will sing together, 'Praise God from whom all blessings flow,'" and this old doxology was sung by the regiment ere we began another day's forced march.

That evening we reached Frog Lake, the scene

of the terrible massacre some weeks before, and by special order slept every man on his arms, as we were reported by the scouts to be surrounded by Indians who might attack us during the night. Next morning Sergt.-Major Lawlor, with a fatigue party, buried the bodies of those who had been massacred there some weeks before. The charred remains of the heroic priests, Fathers Marchand and Fafard, who had thrown themselves between the savage Indians and the whites, were recognized by the beads and crosses they wore, but all the others were little more than indistinguishable ashes. A look around the reserve showed how inexcusable was the rising of the Indians, who were treated so well by a paternal Government, and caused one to feel how utterly devilish was the action of those who by plausible messages had caused these easily excited and merciless savages to bite and destroy the hands that fed them. The reserve, as it lay before us that morning, was one of the most beautiful spots in all the wide country we traversed that year. "Fair as a garden of the Lord," it stretched afar, a flower-flecked prairie, diversified by shady groves and sparkling lakes; but the houses were all burned or wrecked, all implements were destroyed, murder and rapine had made their horrid havoc, and war flags of hideous colors on every side mocked the pure breeze of heaven. Sun-dance lodges were standing there and at several points along our route thenceforward, to overawe the soldiers with evidences of the bravery of those who had taken part in the wild orgies these lodges represented. From their rafters still dangled the cords on which the young braves had hung by hooks in their lacerated flesh till, as they danced wildly around, the portion was torn out, and their recklessness of pain was admitted beyond a doubt. It was a mingled scene that met our gaze as we stood on the shores of Frog Lake that day—a mingled scene of beauty and desolation, reminding us again of the world, still untouched by the Gospel, "where every prospect pleases and only man is vile."

We left Frog Lake and pushed on by a forced march of forty-one miles to Fort Pitt, which our scouts reported the Indians were burning, and which we reached late in the evening only to find the fort (except two buildings) a heap of smoking ruins and the Indians vanished in retreat. As we came down over the brow of the river bank to the fort we found the body of young Cowan, the mounted policeman, who had been killed by the Indians some weeks

INTERIOR OF FORT PITT, JUST BEFORE REBELLION OF 1885.

1. The Worm. 2. The Sky Bird; 3. The Bad Boy (Big Bear's son». 4. Big Bear. 5. Angus Mackay (H. B. Co.). 6. Dufresne (the old H. B. Co. cook). 7. Stanley Simpson (H. B. Co.). 8. Corporal Sleigh (killed at Cut Knife). 9. Trooper Loasby (wounded at Fort Pitt).

before. His body lay naked with face upturned to the open sky. The scalping-knife had not touched his fair hair, but from wounds in the breast it appeared that the Indians, who believe that if they eat a brave man's heart they will get his spirit and courage, had followed that course in the case of the young trooper. They certainly had cause to know of his bravery. He and Constable Loasby had been out from the fort scouting towards Frog Lake, and on their return found the Indians in force along the slope towards the place where their comrades were standing siege. Putting spurs to their horses they made a desperate effort to cut their way through to the fort, but the odds were too great. They were both shot— Cowan dead; but Loasby, whose roan charger we found nearer the fort, was only wounded, and after simulating death awhile to deceive the enemy, he escaped into the stockaded inclosure.

As soon as possible after finding the body of Cowan, his comrades of the Mounted Police dug a grave and reverently buried it, the rattle of their musketry his only funeral requiem, but nothing could more vividly tell the record of a man who worthily wore the uniform of his Queen and died a soldier's death. A few years since, when relating the story of the rebellion, I was glad to hear, from one who stated that he was young Cowan's cousin, that the body thus buried on that lonely bank was exhumed the next winter by order of the young soldier's mother, and taken down to be laid in the place of his father's sepulchre hard by the city of Ottawa.

We hurriedly put in defensible shape the two buildings which remained, left a company of the 65th to hold them, and after a swift march of about eight miles, to a point where two Indians had been shot in a skirmish by Steele's scouts the night before, came within reach of the enemy, as we soon learned definitely by hearing the bullets whistling over our heads. It had been a long chase from the point of starting, but despite all Indian expectations to the contrary, our General had fully made up his mind to "stick to Big Bear's trail" and accomplish the breaking up of his band, if it should take all summer. Hence there was great satisfaction when the routine of the long march was varied on that 27th of May by our coming into contact with the wily and light-footed foe.

CHAPTER XI.

REBELLION AT AN END.

THE place in which we now met the enemy was full of ravines and heavily wooded. The Indians were seen along the top of the hill in front of us, seemingly holding the position. Our little force was thrown into line, with Hatton's scouts to the right and Steele's to the left. On our side the old 9-pounder, which Perry's men had brought from Fort McLeod, opened by sending a shell screaming into the thicket on the hill-top, in a way that must have been extremely unsettling to the nerves of the braves who occupied the place. Then the order came to us to advance, and we rushed forward in skirmishing order, the Indians meanwhile keeping up a scattering fire. We halted for breath, and I remember feeling rather amused at Major Steele, who warned me to take cover, saying, ." If you don't, they will pot you sure," while at the same time he seemed to forget about his own colossal figure seated on a horse seventeen hands high. Once more the bugle broke in with the "Advance," and the line rushed up the hill and over the summit only to find the Indians retreating and leaving us in possession. For some hours we skirmished through the woods, and then our wagon train having come up we camped in the forest for the night.

Humanly speaking, I have never been able to make out why the enemy, who were in force outnumbering us three to one, did not make short work of us in the darkness. The clearing in which we encamped was small and surrounded by dense forest, the wagons were in zareba form with all the men and horses inside, and the night was intensely dark. The Indians must have been already in panic, or, with their knowledge of the situation, they might have rushed in, stampeded our horses, and in the confusion done serious execution. With the sunrise we moved on again, and soon encountered the enemy in a position which a glance showed to the merest amateur to be impregnable to our handful if held by any considerable force. The Indians occupied a steep conical-shaped hill, moated by a deep valley and marshy stream, topped with forest and fortified with rifle-pits, there being, as we afterwards found, no less than five rows of rifle-pits along the ravine by which they expected to be assailed. For some hours the fight was kept up sharply. Our men were in the open, but, strangely enough, only four were wounded, though afterwards many proudly exhibited caps shot through, etc., as evidence of close-enough calls. The enemy were practically invisible, and little could be seen to indicate their presence but the puffs of smoke from their rifles and the "ping" or thud of the bullets around us. About ten o'clock their firing had practically ceased, except for scattering shots from the pits. We afterwards learned the Indians were then in retreat; but the scouts were of opinion that the retreat was a ruse, and that the enemy were coming round behind us (as some of them actually did) to cut off our wagon train and hem us down in the valley.

In a letter I received from General Strange some years afterwards, he said in reference to this engagement: "My force would have gone in to a man, if I had allowed them, but I had the lessons of Fish Creek and Cut Knife before me," implying that he did not feel warranted in risking the lives of his men in a possible trap, against the opinion and advice of the column's "tentacles." So the men were slowly retired by companies till the wagon zareba was reached, when a camp was formed and the wounded men looked after. Word was then sent down the river to General Middleton, at Battleford, for ammunition and reinforcements.

On the day following Major Steele offered to take a flying column and follow the Indian trail, and accordingly, with about fifty picked men out of the Police, the Alberta Rifles and Oswald's scouts, he left camp, accompanied by the "grey team" and wagon with ammunition and supplies. I remember how these fellows—magnificent riders, every one of them—wheeled out on the gallop, and followed where the tracks showed that most of the Indians had gone. We saw no more of them for days, but they kept to the trail and came upon the main body of the Indians at Loon Lake, where a brilliant dash was made upon the enemy, who retired across an almost impassable morass. In this hot, if brief, engagement several Indians bit the dust, and Steele's sergeant-major (Fury by name), and two of the scouts (Fisk and West), were wounded. Fury was very seriously hurt, being shot through the breast and rendered perfectly helpless. Steele's only course, with these wounded men on his hands and no transport or ambulance, was to retire toward the main body, leaving the Indians continuing their journey to the north.

Another of our own companies having come down from Edmonton with much-needed supplies just as Steele left us, we marched back to the scene of our encounter at Frenchman's Butte, only to find that the enemy had vanished, leaving every evidence that they had fled in the wildest panic. The encampment was nearly intact, with the wigwams standing. Great heaps of furs (which went quickly we know not whither), wagons, carts, flour, bacon, cooking utensils, etc., lay around in the greatest disorder, as if they had become of very secondary importance in the race for life. Concerning the furs a good deal has been said even in the sober debates of our Houses of Parliament, but there is not much certainty as to where they were finally bestowed. The staff officers in all the brigades were mightily blamed by those who were themselves angry at not getting a haul, but it is quite likely, according to my observation, that the teamsters, who had the great advantage of receptacles in which to carry parcels, could unfold tales that would exonerate the poor officers from at least a part of the blame.

Standing that day in a pelting rain-storm, we surveyed the position recently held by the enemy and wondered why they had not kept on holding it, so excellently was it suited for standing a long siege. Then going out to the plain beyond we encamped to wait for orders from Middleton, while our scouts tried to locate the scattering trails of the fleeing Indians. While we remained there, several of the white prisoners who had escaped during the fight and confused retreat were brought into camp by the scouts, rejoicing at having regained once more a freedom which they doubtless at times had despaired of ever obtaining, as from day to day hope deferred had made their hearts sick.

Here, too, I remember seeing one of those touches of nature which make the whole world kin. One of the roughest riders and apparently one of the most reckless of the cowboy scouts was seen coming into camp, leading his rougher horse and carrying carefully upon his arm a small wooden box, such as originally might have contained groceries of some kind. At once curious men gathered in a knot at the edge of the camp, and wondered what find Jack (as we will call him) had made. As he approached, one of the men stepped in his way and lifted the cover of leaves, unveiling the wan dead face of a white child some few months old, whose body had thus been reverently coffined and covered by the hand of the mother and left in the woods as the prisoners were dragged along. The man whose curiosity had tempted him to discover the nature of Jack's "find" started to make some contemptuous remark to the crowd, but the scout's eyes flashed such a dangerous fire that the remark stopped short, and the rest made way for that strange funeral procession. Picketing his wild broncho, the scout dug a grave with his own hands, and with a gentleness that would have done that mother's heart good, committed the little body to the ground. After all, we are every one of us under the influence of an unseen world. Perhaps the quiet sympathy Jack had with the unknown mother's grief, or perhaps the tender recollections of child-life as he remembered it, made that rough scout for the time being as gentle as a woman, or it may have been that sometime in an older land he had laid his own dead under the sod, and his heart went back to that God's-acre where a mother was sleeping with their infant child upon her breast.

On the 21st of May, General Strange, feeling that we were close on the enemy, had thought it well to send despatches to Col. Otter at Battleford, acquainting him with the situation, so that, if necessary, a junction could be effected between his force and ours for the hemming in of the Indians and the disposal of the whole question. Two scouts, George Borradaile (now Crofter

Commissioner in Winnipeg) and William Scott (whose present whereabouts I do not know), were selected for the difficult and dangerous enterprise. It was an undertaking requiring both courage and resource, to go down by the river through the enemy's country. A somewhat clumsy boat was the means of travel, and the two scouts made a perilous run in the shadows of night past Fort Pitt, which the Indians were even then setting on fire. When the scouts reached Battleford, General Middleton had arrived there from Batoche. The despatch was delivered, and when next morning the scouts were to return on the south side of the river, Borradaile asked for a revolver, as he had lost his in a mishap by the upsetting of the boat on the way down. The General, much to Borradaile's disgust, said that he himself would go through that country with a stick; but when he did come, as General Strange said, "he brought two infantry regiments, a troop of cavalry, and artillery." The scouts made the return trip safely, though under considerable strain, and reached Fort Pitt again on the 29th of May, the day after our fight at Frenchman's Butte, but in time to take a hand in the Loon Lake expedition.

At this point in our campaign some of our

officers—Capt. Wade, Lieut. Mills and Sergt.-Major Lawlor—left us, being called back to Winnipeg by their duties as government officials. Perhaps there was no man in our regiment so deservedly popular as the sergeant-major, and before he went, though not a man given to speech-making, he responded to the demand of the boys, and bade them farewell in a few words. I can still see the scene before me. It is a dark weird night, with here and there a glimpse of the moon through the rifts of the flying clouds. Near the camp-fire is the wagon which is to carry the officers homeward, and around it the group of red-coats, which includes nearly every man off duty. Beside the wagon, with one hand resting lightly on a wheel, stands the sergeant-major, his tall, powerful figure erect as ever, his grey beard sweeping the broad breast on which glisten, in the flickering light of the camp-fire, three medals, the rewards of his sovereign for services in the Crimea and China. After referring to the long weary marching, and then to the fight which followed, he said that "he was glad that this, probably the last of his many campaigns, had been undertaken with men who had proven themselves of such good stuff as the men of the Winnipeg Light Infantry." It was warm praise from a man who was in the habit of saying only what he meant, and as the wagon drove out and was lost in the darkness, many a poor fellow who had done his best felt his heart swell at the words of the veteran soldier.

While we had been pushing on to this point,

CHIEF POUNDMAKER.

our comrades nearer to the centre of the rebellion had been doing some very active service. A brigade under Col. Otter had, after an exceptionally swift march from Swift Current, relieved Battleford, which had been in a state of siege for months, and then, not without severe loss to themselves, inflicted deserved chastisement on Chief Poundmaker and his marauding

RIEL'S COUNCILLORS IN 1885.

band at Cut Knife. Farther eastward, at the fiery heart of the trouble, General Middleton had captured Batoche, the stronghold of Riel.

The advance from Fish Creek had been carefully made. Batoche was Riel's "last ditch," and after the battle General Middleton himself expressed wonder at the splendid use the rebels had made of the means at their disposal to hold the position. The fight continued for four days, when, the volunteers seemingly growing restive under the protracted manœuvring, made a brilliant charge and carried the position with a rush. The gallantry of all the troops engaged is undisputed, and the list of nine killed and forty-six wounded evidences the keenness of the struggle.

The day after Batoche Riel was found by Scouts Hourie and Armstrong. Hourie took him up on the saddle and brought him into camp, whence he was sent to Regina, with a special guard under Capt. George H. Young, of the Winnipeg Field Battery. There Riel remained through the eventful trial, during which the plea of insanity was raised in vain, and there he was executed on the 16th of November, 1885, meeting his death manfully. His body was given to his friends, and now rests in the graveyard at St. Boniface beneath a granite pillar on which is engraved the single word "RIEL." I was present at the funeral service in the old cathedral, and was deeply impressed by the evident sorrow of the people whose cause he had, with many mistakes, espoused.

TOM HOURIE.

Returning to the field, we find Middleton moving with his column, by way of Prince Albert, to Battleford, where he demanded and received the unconditional surrender of Poundmaker on the 26th of May, the day before our first skirmish with Big Bear. This left the Commander-in-Chief free to move in our direction and effect such a concert with the force under General

Strange as would secure the hemming in and capture of the retreating Indians. Accordingly, Middleton with a strong force came on to Fort Pitt, and leaving his infantry there in camp, reached the point where we were with his mounted men and artillery. There a new plan of campaign was decided on. General Strange's column of infantry was to march northward to the one (as was then supposed) crossing of the Beaver River, while General Middleton, with all the mounted men, was to follow after the main trail of Big Bear and force him up to us at the crossing, where between two fires the matter could soon be settled. Accordingly, we started out next morning to perform our part of the contract, and that night camped at Onion Lake in one of the most terrific thunderstorms I ever witnessed—an amazing and overwhelmingly grand spectacle. The continuous flashing of lightning transformed the prairie with its waving grass into a heaving, tossing sea of flame, while the incessant boom and crash of the thunder, awe-inspiring in the extreme, reminded us of the feeble strength of all earthly force, the puny power of boasted arms before the flash and roar of the artillery of heaven.

All the next day our forced marching was

continued through roads almost impassable and innumerable places where the wagons had to be pulled out by the men, and towards evening Indians were reported ahead near the Beaver River crossing. It was decided to make what became known in the rebellion annals as "the silent march," and so leaving our wagon train, the horses being completely tired out, we started marching again about eight o'clock in the evening. For quite a distance our way was through water knee-deep, and through this swamp I remember how the Frenchmen of the 65th, almost shoeless and half-clad though they were, more than once helped the horses on Perry's gun, next to which they were marching. It was night when we struck the heavy and practically trackless forest, for there was scarcely any trail to be found. The darkness grew denser as we advanced, and the great trees meeting above us shut out the sky. Sometimes in rank, and sometimes in Indian file, we kept on marching in dead silence, with our arms ready for instant use, until about two o'clock in the morning, when a halt was ordered, and by little twig fires—larger were not allowed—we tried to dry our wet and well-nigh frozen garments.

As the day began to dawn we moved on again, and by sunrise arrived at the point near the Beaver River where the Indians had been seen, but found they had vanished. Evidences of their recent presence, however, were at hand, for we found about one hundred bags of flour *cached* in the woods. This was a "windfall," as by this time bread was little more than a distant memory, and even "hard tack" was scarce enough to be appreciated. The brigade supply officer, however, took formal possession of the *cache* of flour, lest the men should get enough to eat for once; but by various devices known to soldiers, such as putting two "kits" in one rubber sheet, and a bag of flour in the other, they rescued a good deal of it from his rapacious clutches, and fared sumptuously, if somewhat secretly, for several days.

Next morning we marched to the Beaver River, where we had orders to wait until General Middleton, whom we left starting out after Big Bear from the scene of our fight, should force him up to us. However, had we done so, we should have had a weary waiting.

The General, following on Steele's trail, met that officer with his command returning from Loon Lake. The wounded were sent back to the main column, and Steele, although his horses and men were much spent, turned back with the General to the scene of the Loon Lake fight. After careful investigation of the ground, Middleton decided that with his guns and heavy horses he could not cross the shaking bog over which the light-footed Indians with their nimble ponies had made their way. He accordingly concluded to turn back, on finding which the Indians also deflected their course, instead of running up to receive our welcome.

In the afternoon of the day we arrived at the Beaver River, No. 1 Company was ordered out under arms to accompany Colonel Smith to the river, about a mile and a half away, to find a suitable crossing should we have to go farther. Here we found another *cache* made by the Chippewyan Indians, filled with articles for priests' wear and church services, which they probably thought they could dispense with while on the war-path. The scenery at this point is very fine. The river, flowing swiftly eastward, is joined by a small stream from the south; the banks are very high and so densely wooded from top to bottom that the foliage seems to be piled in green luxuriance to the very summit. I got permission from the Colonel to take the men down to see the river, and away we went rushing down the steep to the water's edge. There the place is a magnificent natural park. Grand trees, perfectly

straight and with few boughs, tower aloft;
there is no undergrowth, and the whole place is
a perfect picnic-ground. In fact, it so struck
one of our fellows, who remarked, " Boys, this
would be a great place for the people at home
to hold their Sunday-school picnics"; but as
we were then nearly two thousand miles from
home by the route we had followed, we did
not think it necessary to discuss the question
seriously.

On coming again to the top and turning
eastward, the view that met our eyes was marvellously beautiful. The sun, which was slowly
sinking, struck his shafts across the river and
lit the tree-tops beyond. The sunbeams glow-
ing and glinting in mellow radiance on the great
clouds of foliage on the towering banks, the
river flashing and twining in and out through
the forest like some serpent-fish with silvery
scales, the sparkling of the little tributary
stream, of which one could catch glimpses away
down through a veil of green boughs, all
together made up a scene rarely surpassed even
in the great picture gallery of nature. A few
moments we stood gazing on the wondrous view,
and then the word to fall in being given, we
reluctantly left the scene and marched back
to camp.

That night our outlying picket was fired upon, but in the deep darkness and fog nothing could be done except arouse the camp, keep the whole picket under arms, and wait for the day. On that day a band of Chippewyan Indians, with a Roman Catholic priest at their head, came in, and surrendering unconditionally, laid down their arms in a heap at the feet of the General. One could not help feeling sorry for the poor fellows. They did not appear to be a bad lot, but seemed to have been dragged by threats, rather than their own inclination, into rebellion. From the day they surrendered they certainly became a great help to us in many ways, and did their utmost to discover the whereabouts of the bands who still held certain of the white prisoners.

On the next day, Sunday, June 14th, we had service by the Rev. John McDougall inside the zareba. What a motley congregation was there assembled!—some on the wagons, some on the prairie, and some seated on their saddles on the ground. Here a mounted policeman in faded scarlet and gold stood beside a scout with his wide slouch-hat and general air of carelessness; there an infantry man with coat, once red, now like Joseph's—of many colors—sprawled on the grass beside some rough western teamster, whose respect for the minister's cloth kept him quiet, but who, if personally interviewed, might not hesitate to avow heterodoxy in his favorite terse expression, "Difference here, pardner." To the credit of these rough men be it said, I never saw amongst them anything but the most respectful attention to these services, and often one could see their bronze faces light up with a surprising tenderness as they, perchance, recalled the days when they had heard from a mother's lips the same old, but ever new, story of the Cross.

Next day General Strange accepted the offer made by Colonel Smith a few days previously, to take one hundred picked men from the Winnipeg Light Infantry, cross the river and strike northward to a chain of lakes, where he shrewdly, and, as the sequel proved, correctly, thought some of Big Bear's band might have gone with the remaining prisoners. Regimental orders quickly required Companies 1, 2 and 3 to furnish the men, and perhaps the "picking" consisted largely in a selection of those who had some remnants of boots left, and whose uniforms could be counted on as likely to hold together a little while longer.

We (for the writer was fortunate enough to be one of the hundred) were ordered to leave all transport except the Indians' pack-horses, and each man was to carry his own outfit strapped upon his back, as the country through which we were about to travel was impassable to all but foot-soldiers and the nimble pony of the plains. We crossed the river by sections, in two birch canoes, and there left Color-Sergt. Sutherland with a party of five men to build a boat on which to cross the rest of the force if required. We then struck north, and made about five miles that night. Having no tents or other covering, we lay down under the starry canopy of heaven to sleep upon delightful couches of pea-vine on a grassy ridge beside a lake.

Next morning we started at 4.30 without breakfast, as, according to the map, Cold Lake, for which we were striking, was only a few miles distant; but the man who made that map or arranged its scale would have fared ill if he had fallen into the hands of our hungry pack when some hours later Cold Lake was not yet reached. The men marched for the most part in Indian file, threading their way over fallen trees and through mossy swamps, while the Chippewyan Indians (formerly enemies, now our scouts and guides) followed in the rear with the pack-ponies. While passing through a clearing there occurred one of those amusing

incidents which always seemed to come in the
nick of time to relieve the pressure of weariness
and restore the equilibrium of the men. An
Indian pony behind took fright at a tea-kettle
which fell off his back, and which, being tied,
as everything on a pack-horse is, kept hitting
him on the heels. The pony, after having first
kicked vigorously without being able to break
the tough "shagganappi" line, finally came
tearing along our column like a hurricane,
upsetting a captain who had done his best to
get out of the way, and then bowling over a
color-sergeant, who was taken wholly by surprise. The sergeant, who was a middle-aged
and grizzled man, wore his hair very long and
very thick, the military crop not being insisted
on during prairie campaigning, and he was,
moreover, a man of great dignity, polite address,
independent opinions and high-toned bearing.
He was not seriously hurt by the cavalry
onslaught, but in taking his involuntary somersault the pack which he carried on his back
was thrown over his head, to the serious detriment of his toilet, and I can still hear the roar
of laughter that made the woods ring as the
wild tangles of his hair appeared above the
long grass, his face wearing the appearance of
a man caught in a cyclone.

On we plodded, hungry and weary, through the forest, and at length arrived at the lake, which we had almost begun to think was, like the enemy, retiring before us. We hailed with joy the sparkle of water through the trees, and as we neared it the grand repose and the vastness of this lake, so far remote from the haunts of men, struck us with a feeling akin to awe. It stretches away far almost as the eye can reach, the water pure, clear, cold and deeply blue; the beach, stone, gravel and sand, the latter resembling small diamonds; the woods by the shore grand, umbrageous, reflected in the glassy surface. In the stillness of that sunny June day the lake lay before us like some gigantic and marvellous mirror, reflecting the glorious beauty of its Creator's works.

All day long the men were kept busy building willow huts in the woods, as we were to remain here for some time to scout and explore in the surrounding country. I felt, as doubtless did many others, amply repaid for many a weary march by coming to this lovely spot. The evening came down in quiet splendor, the lake lying peaceful and miraged over with the golden, dusky haze of the sunset coolness. Everything seemed as hushed and still as the holy calm of a Sabbath. It was as though conscious Nature, which had shuddered at the deeds of bloodshed and crime enacted on her bosom, was thus prophetically manifesting forth their speedy close and exhibiting in sublime silence the tranquilizing power of that Gospel whose spread in those lonely wilds will put an end to all savagery and woe—that Gospel whose heralding still rings to us across the centuries, "Glory to God in the highest and on earth peace, good-will toward men."

On the 20th of June Indian scouts from our column found the portion of the band that held the McLeans and other prisoners, and on the 23rd, word being conveyed to them to bring these prisoners in, they were sent in all safe and sound to Fort Pitt, being met on the way by Major Bedson and a detachment of the 90th. We now felt that our campaign was practically over, and that we could return with the consciousness of having at least tried to do our duty. We received orders to return to the brigade, our hundred having penetrated farther than any armed force of that time, and accordingly marched back to the Beaver River. There we found that our boat party had completed a large boat, made without a nail and capable of carrying some sixty men. The patriotic souls of the boys had found vent in the launching, for with some compound of axle-grease they had "writ large" across the side the name of their birth-place, the old historic name of Kildonan. There on the Beaver River the 'Kildonan" was left, and there for aught I know it may still remain, a souvenir for the Chippewyan Indians of the sudden and unsolicited visit of the white soldiers to their far-distant fastnesses.

We rejoined our regiment and marched toward the Frog Lake landing of the Saskatchewan, reaching there about midnight, and amidst falling rain crowded aboard the steamer, which passed down the swift-rushing stream to Fort Pitt, where we were warmly welcomed by the 90th of Winnipeg, the Grenadiers of Toronto, and the Midland Battalion. There we ascertained that our regiment, partly for lack of transport, though principally to gather in the outlaw Indians, was to remain behind for a time, but some fifty of us (the campaign being over) got leave of absence, and on the 4th of July, in company with the 65th, the 90th, the Grenadiers and the Midland Battalion, left Fort Pitt for home in three steamers, the *Marquis*, the *Northwest* and the *Baroness*. That day Col. Williams, of the Midland Battalion, who was in the forefront of the charge at Batoche, died on board the steamer *Northwest*, and a private of the 65th, who had been wounded at Frenchman's Butte, died on board the *Baroness*. Only a few days before this I had met Col. Williams at Fort Pitt, being introduced to him

HON. HUGH JOHN MACDONALD, Q.C.

by Capt. Hugh John Macdonald, and was much impressed with his manly appearance and soldierly bearing. He took some kind of fever, and, the facilities for nursing not being of the best, he went down under it with startling suddenness.

The next day we landed at Battleford, a

picturesque though somewhat straggling town on high upland near the river, and at this point we were joined by the Queen's Own Rifles and Ottawa Foot Guards, with the Quebec Battery. Preparations were here made for the funeral of

LIEUT.-COLONEL WILLIAMS.

Col. Williams, whose body was to be sent home overland. It was one of the most impressively affecting and imposing sights I had ever witnessed. The plain board coffin, wrapped in the folds of the old flag under whose shadow he had fought so honorably and well, was lifted on a gun-carriage, behind which a soldier led his riderless horse. His own fine regiment, now going home without a leader, followed as chief mourners, with arms reversed, and the *cortége* numbered fully fifteen hundred armed men. Brass bands were there with muffled drums, and the wild lonely upland echoed the wail of the "Dead March in Saul," as slowly and sadly we conducted the gallant dead to the once beleaguered fort, where within the stockaded inclosure the Revs. D. M. Gordon and Whitcombe held a most impressive service. Many a stern soldier who had stood unmoved amidst dangers gave way to his feelings, many a stalwart form heaved with emotion, and on many a sun-bronzed cheek the tear was seen as we consigned to his last journey one of the heroes in the charge that crushed the centre of rebellion, a man who had passed gloriously through the battle, and who, with a name that will live enshrined in the memory of his country, was returning to his home where loved ones looked for his coming, but had fallen here so suddenly before the grim King of Terrors. Escaping the shot that had ploughed the ranks, he, by a death reached through the gateway of duty, had passed into the unseen, and had added his name to the bead-roll of the slain whose lives were yielded up in sacrifice on the altar of their country.

"The muffled drum's sad roll has beat
   Our soldier's last tattoo,
No more on life's parade shall meet
   That brave and fallen few.
On Fame's eternal camping ground
   Their silent tents are spread,
And glory guards with solemn round
   The bivouac of the dead.
Rest on, embalmed and sainted dead,
   Dear as the blood ye gave;
No impious footstep here shall tread
   The herbage of your grave!
Nor shall your glory be forgot
   While Fame her record keeps,
Or Honor points the hallowed spot
   Where Valor proudly sleeps."

The solemn service over, we boarded our steamers again and moved down the broad stream, passing the ashes of Fort Carlton (burned just after the Duck Lake fight), and stopping a few hours at Prince Albert. Here we saw the place where the people had garrisoned themselves, and also the place where our active enemy, Big Bear, who had been captured a few days before, was held in durance.* There, too,

---

* The old chief after the Loon Lake affair had separated from the band with one companion, and being found by the Mounted Police near the site of Fort Carlton, was taken to Prince Albert. Personally he was rather a harmless old man, and but for two of his band, Wandering Spirit and Little Poplar, would never have been found on the war-path.

we met many old friends of former days, and
as our bands enlivened the day with music
and uniforms were everywhere, the scene was a
brilliant one, broken only by the sadness all
felt as here and there we saw emblems of
mourning worn for the gallant men who from
that place had volunteered to maintain the law
and had laid their bodies on the fatal field of
Duck Lake. In the afternoon we swung out
from our moorings and moved down the river,
the bands playing "Auld Lang Syne" amidst
the cheering of our men, returned by the waving
of innumerable handkerchiefs in the hands of
ladies fair. We made a swift run to the Forks,
where the north and south branches of the
Saskatchewan unite in one gigantic stream, and
at this point we found the hospital barge with
the wounded from Fish Creek and Batoche.
The barge, from which the wounded were then
transferred to one of the steamers, was a model
of cleanliness and comfort, a great credit to the
medical staff and to Nurse Miller, the "Florence
Nightingale" of the rebellion time. The trip
thence was uneventful (save for a storm on
Cedar Lake, which nearly swamped our river
boats), and as we came down the broad bosom of
the magnificent stream we enjoyed the rest, the
meeting with old friends and the telling one

another of "the dangers we had passed," and the story of "how fields were won."

At Grand Rapids, where a horse tramway connects the river with Lake Winnipeg, we left our boats and, passing over to the lake, packed into every corner of the boats and barges there, and reached Selkirk in the early morning of July 15th. There we found many friends awaiting us, and these, notwithstanding our bronzed and bearded faces, recognized us without difficulty and bade us a hearty welcome. After a lunch, provided by the citizens, we boarded our train and reached Winnipeg in the afternoon, exactly three months from the time our regiment had departed for the west.

A magnificent reception awaited the returning troops. The train seemed to push its way through a living mass of men, women and children at the station, and it had scarcely stopped when the cars were besieged by such a throng that the disembarking soldiers could scarcely find room enough to form up. But at length the lines got into some semblance of order, with "Fours, right, quick march" we swung out to Main Street, and as we passed up towards the City Hall beneath arches and banners, and amidst the intense enthusiasm of cheering crowds we saw the genuineness of the welcome and felt amply repaid for all the hardships and dangers of the campaign.

Our own regiment, the Winnipeg Light Infantry, arrived a few weeks later, being the last to leave the field, after receiving the surrender of enemies to five times their own number, amongst them some of the worst Indians in the West, several of whom came under capital sentence at the hands of the country. The regiment had a fitting reception accorded it by the city of Winnipeg, where the equal readiness with which these volunteers had marched through swamps or fought the enemy, as called upon, was duly appreciated, and when No. 1 Company marched down to their former barracks at Kildonan, we were received with Highland hospitality by the kind friends whose goodness had cheered us on the weary campaign, and whose kindness will long be remembered by the boys who went to the front.

The scars left by the rebellion are slowly disappearing, and little else remains but the memory of the manner in which a young nation showed itself ready and able to cope with serious difficulties within her borders. That memory is enough to effectually prevent any such unfortunate movement ever again taking place, and, perhaps, in view of the fact that the pressure of difficulties compacts and solidifies character, it was well that, before sweeping out into the great possibilities that lie before this once "great lone land," it had to pass through such wrestlings as produce a strength never reached on the dead level of uninterrupted ease.

Archbishop Taché.
Archbishop Machray.
Rev. George Young, D.D.
Rev. John Black, D.D.

GROUP OF PIONEER CLERGYMEN.

CHAPTER XII.

RELIGIOUS AND EDUCATIONAL DEVELOPMENT.

WITHOUT religion an individual or a nation is a comparative failure, and without education the means of making the most of our native resources must be largely lacking. Hence it is matter for thankfulness on the part of all who are interested in the West, that the religious and educational work of the country has always had a foremost place in the thought and life of the people. It is a lamentable fact that this has not always been the case in new countries, where the ease with which material prosperity can be attained has often led to more or less serious disregard of the higher life and the institutions which are the hope of humanity. The better state of things in the Canadian West is due principally to two causes. The first is, that the early colonists were of a character and a race always disposed to pay special attention to these things; and the second, that missionaries being early on the ground were able to keep the work of Church and school so well abreast of the country's progress that few, if any, communities to-day are out of touch with these advantages.

In the matter of church work, the Roman Catholics, following the early French explorers, were first on the ground, though their people were not of the colonist but the more nomadic class. Across the Red River from where the city of Winnipeg now stands, this denomination established its headquarters for church and school, near the opening of this century, and named the place St. Boniface. Amongst the early settlers of all creeds their leading men were well known, and often have we heard special mention of Bishop Provencher, a man of magnificent physical mould and statesmanlike ability. It was of his cathedral, with its turrets twain, that Whittier, the Quaker poet, wrote his famous and exceedingly beautiful poem, "The Red River Voyageur," in which he describes the hard voyage of the oarsman in the service of the Hudson's Bay Company, and of the joy that lit up his swarthy countenance as he heard the "bells of St. Boniface" that spoke the message of his home-coming. That cathedral was burned down many years ago, and on its site was reared the present one, from whose tower the bells still ring out their musical chimes.

Some years ago Sir John Schultz (then Lieut.-Governor of Manitoba) reminded the authorities of the cathedral of the birthday of the poet, and asked that the bells be rung in honor of the day. This being done, the Hon. J. W. Taylor, the United States consul at Winnipeg, wrote informing Whittier of the fact. The aged poet, on recovering from an illness with which he was suffering at the time, wrote to Archbishop Taché, at St. Boniface, acknowledging the thoughtful courtesy of the act, and in his letter the following sentences of great beauty occur: "I have reached an age when literary success and manifestations of popular favor have ceased to satisfy one upon whom the solemnity of life's sunset is resting; but such a delicate and beautiful tribute has deeply moved me. I shall never forget it. I shall hear the bells of St. Boniface sounding across the continent and awakening a feeling of gratitude for thy generous act." The letter was scarcely less beautiful than the poem itself, and adds to the halo of romance which the pleasing incident threw around the old cathedral.

As already indicated, Bishop (afterwards

Archbishop) Taché came next in the succession at St. Boniface. He was a man of gentle, lovable disposition, and yet of indomitable will and untiring energy. No man could have exerted a larger control over his own people, and few had wider influence in the country at large. Under his direction missions were extended widely over the whole West, and at St. Boniface the College, which is the principal educational institution of the Roman Catholic Church in the West, was built, so that when the present Archbishop Langevin came into office he found a fully organized and well administered diocese.

Next in the order of their coming into the country is the Episcopal Church, which, partly through the influence of Hudson's Bay Company officials, but mainly by their own enterprise, had a missionary, Rev. John West, on the banks of the Red River in 1820, and this Church continued to be the sole representative of Protestantism in that part of the West until the year 1851, when the Presbyterian Church sent a missionary to the field. This was the more remarkable by reason of the fact that the colony on the Red River brought out by Lord Selkirk was exclusively Presbyterian, and the great majority of that colony remained so, while, to the credit of both missionaries and people,

fully availing themselves of and supporting the
services of the Anglican Church for more than
thirty years The Episcopalians, under Bishop
Anderson, early established a school for boys,
which came to be one of the leading factors in
the life of the country, and which under the
present *régime* of Archbishop Machray, a distinguished educationist, grew into St. John's College, now the principal seat of learning in connection with the Anglican body in the West.
Archbishop Machray deserves more than passing
mention in connection with any reminiscences
of Western history. He is a man of exceedingly
striking appearance, being of gigantic stature
and build, with a strongly-marked and leonine
face. An Aberdonian by birth, he was educated
in his native land and in Cambridge, and it is
generally believed by the students under his
care that what he does not know, especially
about mathematics, is not worth knowing. But
it would be a mistake to suppose that he is only
fitted for residence " within the studious cloisters
pale." He is a man of affairs, who had much to
do with maintaining the equilibrium of the
country in the stormy days of the '69 Rebellion,
and who proved himself so efficient an administrator of church matters in his immense diocese
that he has been honored by the Church with

first place as Primate of all Canada. His influence has been widely felt in educational matters, and especially in connection with the Provincial University, of which he has been Chancellor since its foundation. The missions of the Church of England extend all over the West, and approach about as near to the North Pole as it is possible to do and live. Great dioceses bearing such names as Moosonee, Athabasca and Mackenzie River, give an idea of the far-extended character of this Church's work, and it may be safely said that no denomination has striven more faithfully or more effectively to raise the standard of true living amongst the aboriginal tribes of the North-West.

The third Church to enter this part of the country, as already intimated, is the Presbyterian, whose first missionary, the Rev. John Black, came to the Selkirk colony on the Red River in 1851. For many years he alone upheld the banner of his denomination in the West; then he was joined by the Rev. James Nisbet (who in 1866 founded Prince Albert, on the Saskatchewan), the Rev. Alexander Matheson, William Fletcher, John McNabb and others, till to-day the Presbyterian is the most powerful church organization west of Lake Superior. Its pre-eminent place is due largely to the character of its early missionaries and members, to its educational institutions, and to the splendid organization of its missionary efforts in the newer districts. John Black was a man of great energy, as well as of ripe scholarship, and his people in Kildonan became the pioneers in church extension and also the founders of the educational institutions which have done so much for the Presbyterians, and in which have been trained for various walks in life many from other churches, Protestant and Roman Catholic alike. The parish school at Kildonan fed the demand of the early Scotch settlers for education, and from it Mr. Black outgathered those who sought for higher instruction, until the people's needs demanded a college, and Manitoba College was founded by the Presbyterian Church in 1871. The first professors were the Revs. George (now Dr.) Bryce and Thomas Hart. Dr. Bryce has taken an exceedingly active and vigorous part in all the affairs of the country, and has by voluminous writings contributed much to the diffusion of information as to the West. Prof. Hart is a specialist in classical study, a cultured, gentle and lovable man, who has always exerted marked influence for good on his students. Later on, when the Theological Department of the College was to be strengthened, Revs. Dr. King, the present Principal, and A. B. Baird, men of strong personality and ripe scholarship, were added to the staff. With this staff, assisted by several lecturers in certain branches, Manitoba College has made abundant progress, and has become a strong force in the

REV. GEORGE BRYCE, LL.D.

upbuilding of the new West. This college alone, of all educational institutions of its class, has a summer session in theology in order to provide opportunity for summer study to the students who man the mission fields through the long winter.

Speaking of mission fields brings us to the

work that has been done in the way of keeping abreast with the needs of a growing country in the matter of religious services; and while many men have done much in this regard, the man who, next to the pioneer, deserves to have his name honored, is the Rev. Dr. Robertson, Superintendent of Presbyterian Missions in the North-West. A man of Highland blood, full of intense energy, equally at home in the abode of the millionaire and in the ranch of the pioneer, an indefatigable worker and a powerful pleader in public and private, Dr. Robertson has made an ideal superintendent. He was the first regularly settled pastor of Knox Church, Winnipeg, where he was in charge from 1874 to 1881, when the General Assembly, recognizing the importance of the work and his peculiar fitness for it, appointed him to direct the Home Missionary work of the Church west of Lake Superior. The growth of the Church from three preaching places in 1870 to 840 in 1897 attests the earnestness of the people, and speaks forcibly as to the work done by the Superintendent. As immigration flowed westward over the great plains and through the mountains, the heralds of the Cross were sent onward, the last achievement being the despatching of three missionaries to the Klondike. What has been done in the

Presbyterian Church has been done also in others, though no other man, so far as we know, has been so long in special touch with this particular work as Dr. Robertson.

Where work is to be done one can safely count on finding the Methodist Church in active operation, and so it has proved in the Canadian West. From about 1840 and onward, missionaries of that denomination, Rundle, Evans, Woolsey, George McDougall and others, had been at work farther west, and just before the Rebellion of '69 the Methodist Church in Canada sent the Rev. George Young to begin work in the Red River country. Mr. Young quickly found his way to the heart of affairs, and was eminently successful in laying the foundations of prosperity in a new domain. In the stirring days of the first rebellion, no minister of any denomination exhibited more courage and none had more intimate connection with the unfortunate men who fell under the imprisoning power of Louis Riel. Mr. Young will be especially remembered in the West, not only as the founder of Methodism in Manitoba, but as the man who, after all efforts to secure his pardon were unavailing, was the spiritual adviser of the unfortunate Thomas Scott in his last hours. Since the days of Mr. Young, the missions of the Church have made giant strides, and few places can be found where some of their workers have not gone at some time or other. With the Anglican and Presbyterian churches the Methodists have done much missionary work amongst the Indians, and each of these bodies has charge of Indian Industrial Schools at different points in the country. Under the principalship of Rev. Dr. Sparling, a Methodist college was begun in Winnipeg a few years ago, and now Wesley College, as it is named, possesses one of the most strikingly handsome buildings in the city, and has upon its staff able and influential men.

Other Protestant bodies in the West are the Baptists, who have shown great energy in the extension of their church work, and the Congregationalists, the latter Church only working thus far in the larger centres. Neither of these churches has, as yet, any educational institutions, and hence they are somewhat at a disadvantage in having to draw their trained workers from distant centres.

When we turn to consider the educational system of the country we find remarkable excellence, considering the newness of things. The Province of Manitoba started out with a separate school system, Protestant and Roman Catholic, and this state of affairs continued until 1890, when the famous Greenway-Martin Act was passed, abolishing the separate and establishing a national unsectarian public school system. To recount the controversy that raged around this Act for the six years following would be beyond the purpose of the present writing, and would, in fact, make a literature to the extent of a library. The Roman Catholics claimed that, by a clause in the Manitoba Act providing for the perpetuation of any rights existent, by law or practice, as to denominational schools amongst the people of the country at the time of the transfer, they were entitled to separate schools for all time. Against this people who were familiar with the state of matters when Manitoba entered Confederation could say that if the clause was valid the Episcopalians and Presbyterians had the same rights as the Roman Catholics, and if all pressed their claims a remarkable confusion would soon ensue. It was also said by Mr. Martin, who was the father of the Act of 1890, that if the constitution required the separate school system (which he denied), it would be better in the interests of moulding the people of a new country into one homogeneous mass, to seek amendment to the Constitution rather than perpetuate the double system. Finally, it is now very generally conceded as discovered during the progress of the controversy (if not known for certain before), that the real Bill of Rights as presented by the people of

HON. CLIFFORD SIFTON.
Minister of the Interior; formerly Attorney-General of Manitoba.

the country did not ask for the enactment of the clause above referred to in the form in which it was, after some doctoring, enacted. In any case the Act of 1890 gave great offence to the Roman Catholics, who for the most part persisted in maintaining their own schools out of private subscriptions while paying their taxes like others, and at the same time carrying the case without success through every court in the land, and then to the Imperial Privy Council.

In the process of a few years the Manitoba school question became a public nuisance, inasmuch as it monopolized the attention of politicians and electors all over Canada, to the almost total exclusion of trade and other weighty issues. Hence there was very general relief when the Governments of the Hon. (now Sir) Wilfrid Laurier and of Hon. Thomas Greenway came to a basis of settlement shortly after Mr. Laurier came into power at Ottawa in 1896. The settlement perpetuated the national system of schools, and has been accordingly resisted by the Roman Catholic hierarchy, though many of the people of that Church seem disposed to accept it and come under the operation of the Act and the settlement, which are intended to be enforced in a considerate and conciliatory spirit. The latest development is the somewhat irenic encyclical of the Pope, who adheres to the justice of the claim made by Roman Catholics, and advises continued effort in the course they have been pursuing, but after all practically tells them to take what they can get. Whatever be the intent of the encyclical it is highly probable that with possible slight modifications to render the acceptance of it more agreeable to the Roman Catholics, the system will continue for all time to be in essence a national system of public schools.

HON. F. W. G. HAULTAIN,
Premier of the North-West Territories.

In the North-West Territories the educational system is under the control of a Council of Public Instruction, consisting of the four members of the Executive Committee, *ex-officio*, and four appointed members (two Protestants and two Roman Catholics) without votes. The provisions of the School Ordinance, 1896, in this respect are :—

The members of the Executive Committee of the Territories, and four persons, two of whom shall be Protestants and two Roman Catholics, appointed by the Lieutenant-Governor in Council, shall constitute a Council of Public Instruction, and one of the said Executive Committee, to be nominated by the Lieutenant-Governor in Council, shall be Chairman of the said Council of Public Instruction. The appointed members shall have no vote, and shall receive such remuneration as the Lieutenant-Governor in Council shall provide.

(1) The Executive Committee, or any sub-committee thereof appointed for that purpose, shall constitute a quorum of the Council of Public Instruction, but no general regulations respecting:

- (a) The management and discipline of schools;
- (b) The examination, grading and licensing of teachers;
- (c) The selection of books;
- (d) The inspection of schools;
- (e) Normal training;

shall be adopted or amended except at a general meeting of the Council of Public Instruction duly convened for that purpose.

The following paragraphs from the last report of the Council of Instruction will give further insight into the system:—

"The classes of schools established are Public Schools and Separate Schools. The minority of the ratepayers in any organized public school district, whether Protestant or Roman Catholic, may establish a separate school therein, and in such case the ratepayers establishing such Protestant or Roman Catholic separate school shall be liable only to assessments of such rates as they impose upon themselves in respect thereof. Any person who is legally assessed or assessable for a public school shall not be liable to assessment for any separate school established therein. Provision is made for Night Schools for pupils over fourteen years of age who are unable to attend school during the day.

"Inspectors are appointed by the Lieutenant-Governor in Council, and report to the Council of Public Instruction and the trustees of each district on the scholarship, behaviour and progress of the children, teaching and governing power of the teacher, condition of the buildings, grounds and apparatus, and state of the treasurer's books. They are expected to give any advice and instruction necessary for the successful conduct of the schools. They have nothing to do with religious instruction."

From this it will be seen that the system is a somewhat complex one as compared with that of the Province of Manitoba, where, as indicated already, there is a national unsectarian public school system established, and where an Advisory Board has control under the Government.

D. J. GOGGIN, M.A.

The Superintendent of Education in the Territories is Mr. D. J. Goggin, M.A., a gentleman of large experience and special talents for the work. The comparative smoothness with which the educational machinery of the Territories has been working is due largely to his wisdom and abundant labors.

In the matter of higher education the University of Manitoba, the only degree-conferring body in Arts, is a somewhat unique institution in the educational world. It is constituted by an affiliation of all the denominational colleges in

HON. GILBERT M'MICKEN,

First Agent of Dominion Lands in Manitoba, and one time Speaker of the Local Legislature.

the West, Protestant and Roman Catholic, as well as the Medical College. It is still without buildings, an examining body principally, the teaching except in one or two departments being done in the colleges maintained by the several churches. Notwithstanding this composite character of the institution, the manner of its administration has evidenced such an admirable spirit of mutual good-will, and such an earnest desire to advance the common cause of higher education, that the University has been a signal and unbroken success. All the colleges and the graduates elect representatives, who form the Council, which is the governing body of the University. Altogether we can say, in closing this brief chapter on the religious and educational life of the country, that in an eminent degree for a new land the West furnishes advantages in these directions to all who come within her borders.

As we close this volume and pause a moment to take another look back over the way by which we have come, we are impressed with the marvellously rapid strides that have been taken in the march of the country's progress. Prairies over which not many years ago we have ridden for days in succession without meeting a human being except the roving Indian, or seeing a dwelling other than his wigwam, now are transformed into thriving farms, where in autumn the wheat fields wave and toss like a golden sea. Verily the wilderness has been made glad, and the desert has rejoiced and blossomed like the rose. Railways now run like a network over the once virgin plains, and along the various lines towns have risen from the level sod as if by magic. At these towns, which are growing with a rapidity surprising to anyone who visits them frequently, huge elevators in large numbers receive the finest wheat in the world and send it abroad into ready markets. On the wide plains, once the home of roaming herds of buffaloes, vast numbers of their tamer species feed on the richest grasses, and from every station these cattle are shipped by the hundred to the great food-devouring centres of the world. Away on our Pacific shore the Orient and the Occident stand face to face, and great ships from every quarter of the globe drop anchor in the harbors of our coast cities; while rushing on to the wondrous gold fields, thronging multitudes pass with eager tread. Thus from the isolation of a few years ago has the Canadian West come into touch with the busy haunts of men, and instead of the feeble throbbings of a primitive trade, the blood of a world's commerce, that "calm health of nations," now flows steadily through the giant arteries of a new nation. From what has been related in the closing chapter of this book, it may justly be inferred that those who believe that without religion and education the material greatness of a country is but dust and ashes, are doing their utmost to keep all the nobler ideals of life before the people and uplift the truest standards of success in the presence of all who come into our midst. If Canada knows her opportunity and the day of her visitation, if she holds this vast domain for God and home and truth and purity, there are limitless possibilities of noble endeavor and high achievement before us.

www.ingramcontent.com/pod-product-compliance
Lightning Source LLC
Chambersburg PA
CBHW020758230426
43666CB00007B/756